# DVD Production

# DVD Production
## A practical resource for DVD publishers

**Philip De Lancie and Mark Ely**

Focal Press

OXFORD  AUCKLAND  BOSTON  JOHANNESBURG  MELBOURNE  NEW DELHI

Focal Press
An imprint of Butterworth-Heinemann
Linacre House, Jordan Hill, Oxford OX2 8DP
225 Wildwood Avenue, Woburn, MA 01801-2041
A division of Reed Educational and Professional Publishing Ltd

A member of the Reed Elsevier plc group

First published 2001

**British Library Cataloguing in Publication Data**
De Lancie, Philip
   DVD production
   1. DVD technology
   I. Title     II.  Ely, Mark
   621.3'97'67

**Library of Congress Cataloguing in Publication Data**
A catalogue record for this book is available from the Library of Congress

ISBN 0 240 51611 7

Composition by Genesis Typesetting, Laser Quay, Rochester, Kent
Printed and bound in Great Britain by Clays Ltd, St Ives plc

# Contents

Contents

# Preface

Since its introduction in the autumn of 1996, DVD has been growing at an astronomical rate. By far the most successful launch ever of a consumer electronics format, the adoption of DVD has outpaced that of CD, VHS, and LaserDisc. At the same time, the format is on-target to surpass the Compact Disc as the dominant optical storage format on new personal computing platforms by 2002. With its unique ability to bridge the consumer electronics and computing industries, DVD will become the standard physical delivery medium for digital video, audio and data. Additionally, DVD's ability to integrate with the Internet will enable powerful synergy between the rich media experience of DVD and the immediacy and interactivity of the Web.

With the finalization of the DVD-Audio specification, DVD is now a family encompassing six closely-related formats: DVD-ROM, DVD-Video, DVD-Audio, DVD-Recordable (DVD-R), DVD-Random Access Memory (DVD-RAM), and DVD-Rewritable (DVD-RW). While DVD-Video was the first of the DVD formats to grab the attention of consumers, DVD-ROM has found ready acceptance in the personal computing market, and the more recently introduced DVD-RAM format is also catching on. DVD-R, meanwhile, has established itself as an attractive medium for professional applications such as presentations and kiosks.

With both DVD-Audio and DVD-RW debuting at the consumer level in 2000, the future looks bright for DVD's continued growth. As a medium for storing and playing back digital video and audio information, DVD is unprecedented in its flexibility and its possibilities. In the coming years we may find that DVD becomes an alternative to tape for video and audio recording in the home, as well as in professional production environments.

If you are interested in creating content for DVD, or simply wondering what DVD has to offer, this book will give you insight into the DVD format, its

**Preface**

history and technical details, as well as an illustration of real-world DVD production processes. Whether you are a video professional, an audio mastering engineer, or a content publisher, sooner or later DVD will likely be a part of your business. With that in mind, we hope you will find the following both informative and helpful.

# About the authors

**Philip De Lancie** is a freelance writer covering technology and market developments for production professionals in fields such as video, film, audio, interactive multimedia, and the Internet. He has written extensively on topics including DVD, surround sound, streaming media, and High-Definition video. Since 1985 De Lancie has been published regularly in *Mix*, where he is the New Technologies Editor. He is also a contributing writer for *Millimeter*, and a frequent contributor to magazines including *EMedia*, *Video Systems*, *NetMedia*, and *Digital Video* (*DV*). His work has also been published in *NewMedia*, *Post*, *Electronic Musician*, and *WEBTechniques*. De Lancie's writing draws on his own professional experience in audio engineering, including 13 years in CD premastering, as well as in multimedia production for the Web and CD-ROM.

**Mark Ely** is Vice President of Business Development and Strategic Planning at Sonic Solutions, the world's leading provider of DVD authoring and publishing applications. In 1995 Mr Ely helped to design and develop the first commercially available DVD authoring system, Sonic DVD Creator, and has been instrumental in bringing Sonic's subsequent award-winning DVD production technology for corporate video professionals and consumers to market. Mr Ely has a background in product marketing, digital video compression technology, high-speed networking, CD-audio mastering and digital audio system design.

# Disclaimer

This book deals with issues of emerging and rapidly changing standards and technologies. Readers are cautioned that the information it contains is subject to change without notice.

All information included in this book is based on sources believed to be reliable, and is believed to be accurate as of the date of publication (December 2000). However, neither Sonic Solutions nor its affiliates will be liable for any damages, including indirect or consequential, from the use of this document, or reliance on the accuracy of the information contained in this booklet.

Sonic Solutions, SonicStudio, SonicStudio HD, Sonic DVD Creator, and Sonic DVD Fusion and DVDit! are trademarks of Sonic Solutions. Other trademarks are the property of their respective owners.

# Part I

## DVD formats

# Chapter 1

# The DVD story

## Before DVD

The origin of DVD lies in the first broadly successful optical format – the Compact Disc. Since the introduction of the audio Compact Disc in 1982 and the CD-ROM in 1985, the CD has become a universally accepted carrier for music, data, and multimedia entertainment. CD-Audio was by many measures the most successful new consumer entertainment format of its time. CD-ROM has enhanced and enabled many aspects of the desktop computer revolution, and is now included as a standard item on most desktop and laptop PCs (although they are quickly being replaced with CD-compatible DVD-ROM drives).

Since the CD first appeared, consumer electronics and CD manufacturing companies have been working on new techniques to boost both the storage capacity (74 minutes or 650 Megabytes (Mbytes)) and the data transfer rate (1.4 Megabits per second (Mbps)) of the format. In 1993, Nimbus Technology and Engineering announced the first double-density CD format, which supported two hours of MPEG-1 video playback. This was the first demonstration that CD technology could carry high-quality video as well as audio, and suggested that a new format might be on the horizon.

By 1994, cable, satellite, and video-on-demand services were making strong inroads into the home video entertainment market, competing for the consumer's time and money. Responding to the potential erosion of revenues from VHS sales and rentals, the home video industry recognized the need for a new consumer video format that would deliver superior picture and sound quality. Encouraged by the CD's role in revitalizing the

**Table 1.1** Initial studio requirements for an optical video format.

High-resolution video (CCIR-601 broadcast standard)
133-minute movie to fit onto one side of a high-density disc
High-quality audio – stereo and six or more channels of surround sound
Three to five language streams
Up to 30 subtitle streams
Copy protection
Parental lock for adult-oriented titles
Multiple aspect ratio – 16:9 wide-screen; 4:3 pan-scan and letterbox

record industry, major Hollywood film studios formed an advisory committee to define a set of requirements for a similar optical video format.

The committee's recommendations are listed in Table 1.1.

By January of 1995, two prototype formats emerged: the Super Density (SD) format proposed by Toshiba and a consortium of partners, and the Multimedia Compact Disc (MMCD) proposed by Philips and Sony.

With the prospect of a 'Beta versus VHS' format war looming on the horizon, and under pressure from the studios and computer companies, the consumer electronics manufacturers reached a general agreement in December 1995. They formed the DVD Consortium to agree upon a single, unified specification for their next-generation video format. (The original members of the DVD Consortium were Hitachi, JVC, Matsushita, Mitsubishi, Philips, Sony, Thomson Multimedia, Time Warner, and Toshiba.) The Consortium then created a number of committees or 'working groups', each responsible for one aspect of the new format (physical construction, data organization, etc.).

# The formats emerge

While video playback was the original inspiration for the new optical format, DVD Consortium members knew that the expanded capacity and higher data rates of DVD made the new format well suited for many other applications. In addition to working on the underlying DVD-ROM format, on which the DVD-Video would be built, the Consortium envisioned a third read-only variant which could serve as an eventual replacement for the venerable Audio CD. It also defined physical variations, DVD-Recordable and DVD-Rewritable, to allow for different types of recording.

In light of all the possible uses for optical media storage systems, the specifications for DVD were divided into several 'books', designated A to E. The DVD Forum later added a Book F. The DVD books are listed in Table 1.2.

**Table 1.2** DVD books A to E.

| | |
|---|---|
| A | DVD-ROM (Read-Only Memory) |
| B | DVD-Video |
| C | DVD-Audio |
| D | DVD-R (Recordable) |
| E | DVD-RAM (Random Access Memory) |
| F | DVD-RW (Rewriteable) |

Recalling how the acceptance of the CD-ROM format had been slowed by compatibility problems between its various flavours (CD-I, Video CD, Macintosh CD-ROM, ISO-9660 CD-ROM, Photo CD, Hidden data track CD-Audio), the DVD Consortium decided to unify the entire family of DVD formats with a common file system. This new UDF (Universal Disc Format) file system was designed to play back in any computer system and to accommodate writeable and re-writeable variations. With UDF support included on virtually all computer operating systems, any computer with a DVD-ROM reader would be able to access data on a DVD disc, be it DVD-Video, DVD-Audio or the DVD-ROM format.

# A dramatic launch

The Version 1.0 specifications for the physical, logical and video parts of the read-only disc (DVD-ROM) were published in September 1996. After finalization of copy protection methods, DVD-Video was introduced into the Japanese market in late 1996, into the North American market in 1997, and into European market in early 1998.

DVD-Video's growth since its introduction has been dramatic. The following chart compares player shipments for new consumer electronics formats in the years following each format's introduction.

With year-to-year percentage increases in the number of DVD-Video players sold running in the hundreds, the format enters the new century with an installed base of some eight million worldwide. However, DVD player sales only tell part of the story, because DVD-Video titles will also play back on computer-hosted DVD-ROM drives. Roughly 50 million DVD-ROM drives had been shipped by the end of 1999, and it is estimated that by 2002 more than 90 million will be shipped annually.

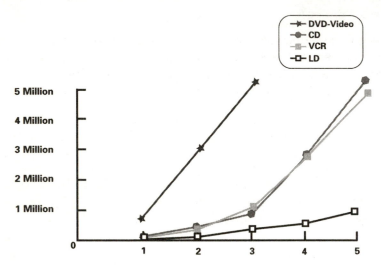

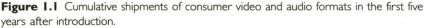

**Figure 1.1** Cumulative shipments of consumer video and audio formats in the first five years after introduction.

# DVD-Audio

In January 1996, the first meeting was convened of the DVD Consortium's Working Group-4, which is responsible for the DVD-Audio standard. Working Group-4 solicited input from the music recording industry via the trade associations that represent the world's major recording companies: the Recording Industry Association of America (RIAA), the International Federation of the Phonographic Industry (IFPI), and the Recording Industry Association of Japan (RIAJ). In response to the Working Group-4 request, these groups formed the International Steering Committee (ISC) to coordinate their input into the DVD standards-setting process.

The ISC met with Working Group-4 in May of 1996, commencing a series of meetings and evaluations that would take more than 18 months. During this time the DVD Consortium was enlarged to become the DVD Forum, now made up of more than 100 member companies. (Sonic Solutions is a voting member of the DVD Forum, as well as a member of several working groups, including Working Group-4.)

At the first meeting, the ISC delivered to Working Group-4, a set of technical requirements. Chief amongst these were that the new format support uncompressed high-resolution digital audio; that it allow both stereo and surround sound channel configurations; that it incorporate not only audio but also video and data elements; and that it offer copyright and anti-piracy protections.

Working Group-4 published a draft specification of the new audio format for its members at the end of November 1997. The official Version 0.9 specification was subsequently published in May 1998. To maintain continuity with the CD-Audio format, these specifications required that DVD-Audio players also play Audio CDs.

At the same time, because of certain requests made by the ISC to Working Group-4 in the spring of 1998, a number of changes were made to the DVD-Audio specification. Most notably, to make sufficient room on the disc for longer programs of high-resolution, multichannel sound, the ISC requested that player support be mandated for a 'lossless' (output identical to input) compression scheme. Various systems were evaluated, and Meridian Lossless Packing (MLP) was chosen for inclusion in the specification.

The Version 1.0 DVD-Audio specification has now been published, and the process of launching the format worldwide is taking place throughout 2000 and 2001.

# Super Audio CD

Super Audio CD (SACD) is built on the physical and logical foundation as the DVD specification (same disc size and file system). Like DVD-Audio, it is intended to support high-fidelity delivery of both stereo and multichannel sound. Super Audio CD, however, is based on the Direct Stream Digital (DSD) audio coding technique.

Unlike PCM encoding (the encoding technique used for the CD and in the DVD-Audio specification), DSD does not attempt to measure the amplitude of an analog wave at discrete points in time (44 100 times per second for a CD, for instance). Rather, it measures whether a wave is rising or falling, and it does so at a sampling rate (2.8 million times per second, or 2.8 MHz) that is many times higher than the rates used for PCM. This technique based on over-sampled changes in the amplitude of an audio signal ('delta-sigma' encoding) has some very attractive properties. For instance, quantization noise is confined for the most part to areas of the audio spectrum where it is imperceptible to the human ear.

Sony and Philips originally proposed DSD for inclusion in a future consumer audio recording format. The companies subsequently developed and proposed a new read-only disc format –Super Audio CD – to the content holders, publishers, and replicators who make up the community of Compact Disc licensees.

Version 1.0 of the Super Audio CD specification has now been published as the 'Scarlet Book' (a reference to CD-Audio's 'Red Book'), and a two-channel version of the players was released in Japan in the late spring of 1999. In the US, a combination DVD-Video/SACD (two-channel) player has been announced by Sony and a multichannel SACD player announced by Philips, both scheduled for shipment late in 2000.

At the time of this writing, the precise relationship between Super Audio CD and DVD-Audio is still somewhat unclear. There have been some suggestions that DSD be included in DVD-Audio, but to date DSD playback support has not been mandated by the DVD Forum. There is, however, a 'data definition area' designated in the DVD-Audio specification as 'reserved for future use', leaving the door open to future inclusion of DSD as an optional coding technique for DVD-Audio. Additionally, there have been some very specific statements by members of the Super Audio CD group that DVD-Audio player manufacturers are completely free to incorporate Super Audio CD support into their players. Thus it is entirely possible that next-generation players will be built to accommodate playback of DVD-Audio and Super Audio CD, in addition to CD (required of every DVD player) and, probably, DVD-Video (see the discussion of Universal players in Chapter 5).

Further discussion of Super Audio CD is beyond the scope of this book.

# Chapter 2

# DVD physical specifications

## Comparison with CD

While the surface area of a single DVD layer is the same as that of a CD, technical advances in both optical media and digital processing algorithms give the DVD layer more than seven times greater data capacity. This greater capacity is achieved in part by reducing the size of the 'pits' used to mark the data on the disc surface, so that more pits fit in a given area. Increased pit density means more available bits. And with a more efficient error correction scheme, DVD needs to reserve fewer bits for data redundancy, allowing more overall material to be stored on the disc.

**Table 2.1** Media specifications of the DVD and CD systems.

|  | DVD | CD |
|---|---|---|
| Disc diameter | 120 mm (5 in.) | 120 mm (5 in.) |
| Disc thickness | 1.2 mm (2 bonded 0.6-mm layers) | 1.2 mm |
| Track pitch | 0.74 pm | 1.6 pm |
| Laser wavelength | 650 or 635 nm red laser | 780 nm red laser |
| Numerical aperture | 0.60 | 0.45 |
| Minimum pit length | 0.4 pm | 0.83 pm |
| Error correction | RS-PC | CIRC |
| Signal modulation | B-16 (EFM+) | B-14 (EFM) |
| Reference scanning velocity | 3.49 m/s (single layer) | 1.2 to 1.4 m/s |
|  | 3.84 m/s (dual layer) |  |
| Data capacity | 4.7 to 17 Gigabytes | 650 Megabytes |
| Maximum data rate | 10.00 Mbps | 1.4112 Mbps |

# Capacity

We refer above to DVD 'layers' because the physical construction of a DVD is quite different from that of a CD. While a CD is always a single piece of moulded polycarbonate, DVD can be manufactured in at least four different physical variations, each with a different data capacity. All of these variations are made up of two polycarbonate platters (substrates) bonded back-to-back. The finished thickness of these discs is the same as that of a CD, but the double-sided manufacturing technique increases the rigidity of the media and minimizes warpage.

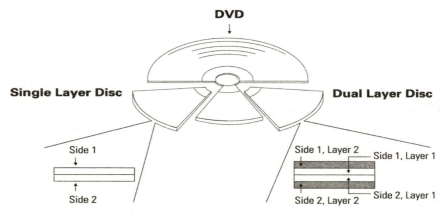

**Figure 2.1** Physical structure of a DVD disc.

DVD's disc configurations are referred to by their capacities in Gigabytes (GB), rounded (for the sake of convenience) up to the next whole number. In the world of computers, a Gigabyte would mean a million kilobytes of 1024 bytes each. However, in the case of DVD, data capacity and data rate are measured in simple multiples. For example, a kilobyte equals 1000 bytes

**Table 2.2** Capacity of DVD disc configurations.

| DVD size | Number of sides | Number of layers per side | Capacity (billion bytes) |
|---|---|---|---|
| DVD-5 | 1 | single | 4.70 |
| DVD-9 | 1 | dual | 8.54 |
| DVD-10 | 2 | single | 9.40 |
| DVD-18 | 2 | dual | 17.08 |

(not 1024 bytes), a megabit equals 1 000 000 bits, and 1 GB means one billion bytes.

As shown in Table 2.2, the base-case DVD – a single-sided/single-layer disc – has a capacity of 4.7 GB, and is called a DVD-5. For DVD-Video titles requiring greater capacity, several other configurations are currently in use. DVD-9 discs (single-sided/dual layer) allow direct access to all the data stored on both layers, while DVD-10s (double-sided/single-layer) are two discrete discs, requiring that the DVD be turned over to access information on the other side. The largest capacity discs are DVD-18s (double-sided/double-layer), which are effectively two discrete DVD-9 discs in one. And at least one replicator, Warner Advanced Media Operations, is also offering a DVD-14 configuration (dual layer on one side, single layer on the other) which was not anticipated in the DVD specification.

# Mixed-density dual-layer discs

One of the requirements originally considered for DVD-Audio was that discs in the new format be playable on existing CD players. A frequent topic of discussion in ISC/WG-4 meetings was the possibility of achieving this with a mixed density disc. Based on the dual-layer technology developed for DVD, these discs would combine a conventional CD layer with a semi-transparent layer containing high-density DVD information. The idea was that the disc would play from the CD layer if placed in a conventional CD-Audio player, while playing the DVD-Audio program when played in a DVD-Audio player.

To date, no one has announced any plans to manufacture or release a product combining a CD layer and a DVD-Audio layer into one disc. One

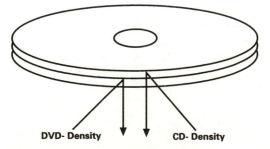

**Figure 2.2** Physical structure of a mixed-density DVD disc.

complicating factor is that the charter of Working Group-4 did not extend to specifying player capabilities (which is the province of another working group). Another problem is that, at least at the present time, the cost to manufacture a mixed density disc is significantly greater than the cost of manufacturing a single layer DVD disc, and this cost in turn is quite a bit greater than the cost of manufacturing a conventional CD.

While it is certain that manufacturing costs for DVD disc replication and dual-layer replication will fall, it is unlikely that these will approach the cost of conventional CD manufacturing for quite some time. That makes it unlikely that a mixed-density disc with a CD layer will be incorporated into DVD-Audio anytime in the near future.

# Chapter 3

# DVD-ROM: the foundation of DVD

## Logical format and UDF file system

All DVD formats – DVD-Video, DVD-Audio and Super Audio CD – are based on the DVD logical format. This is a key point differentiating DVD from the CD family, in which CD-ROM is a separate format from CD-Audio. Every DVD disc is a DVD-ROM disc and can be interpreted as a set of computer-readable files. The corollary of this is that every DVD-player is, to at least some degree, a computing device capable of reading a file system and performing various actions in response to the data found in the files.

The file system used in DVD is Universal Disc Format (UDF). UDF was designed specifically for optical media and is an evolution of the ISO-9660 format that became a standard for CD-ROM applications after the initial years of confusion. UDF defines how the file system is implemented to facilitate use in an optical, replicated format, and to permit use with DOS, OS/2, Macintosh, Windows and UNIX operating systems.

As used in DVD, the UDF file system is constrained to a specific logical sector size (2048 bytes). DVD-Video imposes a number of additional constraints to facilitate the use of the file system in an inexpensive playback device, such as a set-top player. These constraints, contained in an appendix to the OSTA specification, are referred to as 'micro-UDF'.

# Content zones

Like CD-ROM, DVD-ROM is a large information container that may be used to store a vast array of applications and files in a variety of formats, including text and word processing documents, database and spreadsheet files, multimedia presentations, digital audio, graphics and video, HTML pages, and browsers supporting Web connectivity. Thus, storing content for DVD-Video and DVD-Audio playback is only one aspect of DVD-ROM's overall utility.

To ease implementation in inexpensive players, the DVD specifications include predefined directory locations on DVD-ROM discs for DVD-Video and DVD-Audio use. DVD-Video players look for all of their data in a 'Video_TS' directory, whilst DVD-Audio players can look in both Video_TS and 'Audio_TS' directories.

Material on a DVD that is stored outside of these directories is said to reside in the 'DVD-Others zone' of the disc, and is effectively invisible to a DVD-Video or DVD-Audio player. Such material is, however, completely accessible to a computer-hosted DVD-ROM drive. Because all DVD formats are based on DVD-ROM, DVD offers the ability to create hybrid discs that play back on inexpensive DVD-Video and DVD-Audio devices, whilst simultaneously delivering added-value material in computer-based settings.

**DVD Drive**

**Figure 3.1** An internal DVD-ROM drive installed in a computer.

# DVD-ROM readers

All DVD-ROM readers (drives) will also read CD-ROM discs. To play a DVD-Video title in a DVD-ROM-equipped computer, the machine must not only include a DVD-ROM drive, but also have the ability to decode the audio and video formats mandated in the DVD-Video specification. At the time of this writing, virtually all personal computer manufacturers, including Apple, Compaq, Dell, Gateway, IBM, Hewlett-Packard, NEC, Sony, and Toshiba are offering DVD-Video capable models.

The complexity of DVD-Video's video and audio formats means that decoding and output operations can place substantial demands on the computational resources of a computer. Initially most PC manufacturers elected to use hardware-based DVD decoding technology, but with today's extremely fast CPUs (often optimized for multimedia), it is possible for DVD content to be processed in software alone, or using 'hardware-assisted software' decoding. Consumers upgrading existing PCs, however, are generally sold DVD-specific hardware decoding kits that are based on an add-in card.

Just as computer-hosted playback solutions became available for DVD-Video as that format took off, DVD-Audio solutions should begin to appear in 2001 as the new format is launched.

# Web connectivity and eDVD™

As described in the previous section, the presence of zones on a DVD disc allows the design of hybrid titles, which give users with DVD-ROM drives access to additional content that is not in DVD-Video or DVD-Audio format. Among the most popular uses of hybrid titles is Web connectivity, where an application is included in the DVD-Others zone (a custom browser, for instance) that has the capability to dial up the publisher's Web site. This allows a DVD publisher to link media content stored on a disc (motion video, audio, graphics) with additional dynamic content (updated information) delivered over the Web.

With a Web-connected DVD, the user essentially gets the best of both worlds: a rich multimedia environment (from the DVD) and up-to-the-minute information (from the Web). A DVD-Video concert title, for instance, might include a browser that, when launched in a DVD-ROM drive, automatically links the user to the concert artist's section on a record label website. The section could include tour information, samples of songs from the artist's recordings, and merchandise such as CDs, T-shirts and posters. The site might also include a chat area for the artist's fans, a schedule of special Web-cast interviews with the artist, and preview tracks from upcoming releases.

While the user's activities with a browser stored in the DVD-Others zone of a disc could be separate from actually watching content (a movie, for instance) stored in the DVD-Video zone, the benefit to the user may be enhanced by integrating the content from the two zones into a single experience. Sonic's eDVD™, for example, allows DVD-Video to play back from a page in a Web browser, and lets the author of the DVD create links between the DVD-Video content and other elements of the page.

**Figure 3.2** Using eDVD links, a window containing content from a DVD-Video title plays back from a Web page displayed in a browser.

Applications for eDVD exist in both entertainment and corporate/institutional markets for DVD. A historical drama, for instance, might include links to a Web site offering news accounts and interviews with those who participated in the actual events depicted in the movie, or to a commerce site with books on the same subject. A sales presentation with full-screen video and surround sound could play inside a Web browser from a page that also links to an online product information database and order-taking system, allowing a salesperson in the field instantly to place an order as they close a deal. Or a training program might integrate browser-based text and form-based (HTML) quizzes with rich audio-visual demonstrations.

By facilitating synergy between the media-rich environment of DVD and the flexible, up-to-the-minute interactivity of the Web, eDVD expands the interactive design possibilities of hybrid DVDs. The eDVD technology works directly with the operating-system-specific implementations that support DVD playback on computers. On the Microsoft Windows platform (Windows 98 and higher), eDVD acts via the DirectShow applications programing interface (API). On Mac OS computers, DVD-Video can be played from an eDVD Web page, but the video is displayed in the standard Apple DVD player, outside of the browser window.

# DVD extensions: sDVD™, cDVD™, and hDVD™

The fact that all members of the DVD family are DVD-ROMs at heart is what allows the integration of content on a DVD-Video or DVD-Audio title with content on the Web, effectively extending the capabilities of DVDs used in a computer-hosted context. The flip side of this concept – using DVD to extend the capabilities of the Web – is the idea behind Streaming DVD (sDVD™).

With sDVD, the contents of a DVD-Video title are freed from the requirement of residing on a DVD disc. Instead, the source assets are data-reduced to bit rates tailored for streaming over networks. The sDVD streams retain the interactivity of the original DVD content, but are viewable over broadband Internet connections and intranets.

The data-reduction process is handled by authoring tools from Sonic Solutions. Once authored, sDVD content may be published on the Internet through an FTP upload to a standard web server, or streamed directly from the desktop using a Sonic utility called PersonalBroadcaster™. To read sDVD content, the computer uses a PC-based DVD player application.

While sDVD brings DVD-style presentations to networks, another DVD extension enables DVD-Video content to be played back on computers equipped with CD-ROM rather than DVD-ROM drives. Dubbed cDVD™, the technology uses CD-ROM discs – pre-recorded or CD-Rs – which are formatted as DVD-Video discs.

For programing that requires only the capacity of a CD-ROM (650 MB), cDVD will allow DVD-Video content to reach computer users who are not yet equipped with DVD-ROM drives. Since DVD-ROM drives also read CD-ROMs, the same discs are also playable on DVD-ROM equipped computers (although not in current set-top DVD-Video players). cDVD playback requires a software-only DVD player, which is automatically embedded in the DVD-Others zone of a cDVD by authoring tools from Sonic Solutions.

**DVD Production**

A third extension to DVD is hDVD™, which expands the video capabilities of DVD to include all formats supported by the ATSC DTV standard, not only Standard Definition (SD) but also High Definition (HD). Therefore, DVD may be used for computer-based delivery of video in formats such as 720p and 1080i (p: progressive video; i: interlaced video), with all the interactivity and functionality of a regular DVD-Video title. The amount of HD material that may be stored on an hDVD depends on the resolution of the video format used. hDVD authoring capabilities are available in authoring tools from Sonic Solutions, while hDVD-capable software DVD players handle the playback of hDVDs on computers.

# Chapter 4

# DVD-Video: home video and beyond

As described earlier, DVD-Video was developed as a consumer format for high-quality video playback from set-top players connected to TVs. However, the format's feature set also includes support for extensive interactivity, which makes DVD-Video attractive not only for home viewing of feature films, but also for applications such as music videos, games and karaoke. In corporate and institutional settings, meanwhile, DVD-Video is catching on rapidly as the preferred delivery solution for presentations, catalogs, training and education materials, kiosks, and point-of-purchase displays.

## DVD-Video players

All DVD-Video players have the ability to read each of the DVD physical configurations from DVD-5 to DVD-18. A single disc image may not extend over two sides of the same disc (on DVD-10, for instance), but may extend over two layers on the same side of a disc (as in DVD-9). This means that for long movies the data may extend across two layers, allowing the user to view the entire program without having to flip the disc.

DVD-Video players are all required to be able to play CD-Audio discs. Of course, conventional CD players are incapable of playing DVD-Video discs. Depending on the manufacturer, DVD-Video players may also include support for VideoCD, but this is not a required element of the DVD specification.

# User interface

The user interface for DVD-Video players is a remote control. All DVD-Video player manufacturers are required to provide similar keys and functionality on their remotes. These include: Play, Stop, Pause, Next program, Previous program, Title (main) menu, root (Title Set) Menu, Up, Down, Left, Right, Enter, and Return. Additionally, remotes must include a numeric keypad for number entry, although this may be hidden in an access panel within the remote control.

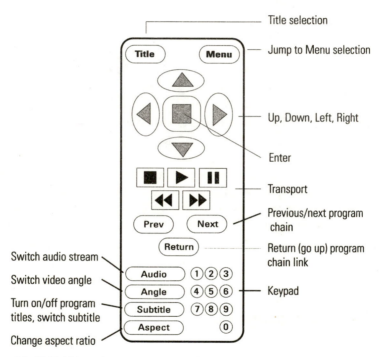

**Figure 4.1** DVD-Video player remote control.

# Video playback

## The MPEG format

Raw (uncompressed) digital video requires enormous disc space to store and ultra-high data bandwidth (bit-rate) to play back. DVD is only able to store more than two hours of video on a single layer because the specification supports playback of video that has been compressed.

One aspect of video compression involves a more efficient storage of information – both within individual video frames and between a series of consecutive frames – that is redundant. Another aspect involves discarding information from the source signal that is judged to be least important from the standpoint of re-creating a quality image during playback. Together, these two approaches are used to reduce the overall volume of data.

Both MPEG-1 and MPEG-2 video compression schemes (developed by an international organization called the Motion Picture Experts Group) are supported in DVD-Video. MPEG-1 is an earlier technology that is still used in Video CD (White Book). But advances in digital signal processing algorithms subsequently made MPEG-2 possible, which is universally regarded as yielding higher image quality. MPEG-2 also supports advanced features such as variable encoding rates, progressive or interlaced frames, and runtime 'pan/scan' of widescreen images.

MPEG-2 encoding is the norm for most DVD-Video titles. Depending on the bit-rate employed, the image quality of video that has been professionally encoded in the MPEG-2 format may be virtually indistinguishable from that of the uncompressed video source.

The structure of MPEG-2 video will be covered in greater detail later, when we look at the process of encoding video for DVD. For now, it is enough to know that MPEG-2 video may be encoded in either Constant Bit-rate (CBR) or Variable Bit-rate (VBR) modes. In CBR, bits are allocated evenly across the entire program. In VBR, more bits are allocated to complex, hard-to-encode segments of the program, and fewer to the rest. If artfully done, VBR encoding results in higher subjective playback quality at lower overall bit-rates. VBR's advantages are greatest when encoding program material of about one hour or longer.

Depending on the country in which a DVD-Video title is released, the video material will be stored for playback in either NTSC or PAL format, the two main systems used worldwide for television signals. These systems use two interlaced fields to make up a complete picture or frame of video, with odd lines scanned in one field and even lines scanned in the next. NTSC uses 30 frames (60 fields) per second, each with 525 lines, of which 480 are used for picture information. PAL uses 25 frames (50 fields) of 625 lines, with 576 lines of picture information.

Player manufacturers are not required to support both NTSC and PAL DVD discs in a single player, although in practice most PAL players also support NTSC. If a title is to be distributed in both NTSC and PAL

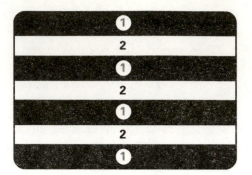

**Figure 4.2** In interlaced video, a complete frame is made up of two fields, each of which scans every other line (odd lines in pass 1, even in pass 2).

countries, either separate releases will be prepared for each format, or a disc will be created with PAL content on one side and NTSC content on the other (assuming the program will fit on one side of a disc). Alternatively, an NTSC version may be distributed under the assumption that most viewers in PAL countries will be able to play it back.

## Aspect ratios

Early in the development of motion pictures, the film industry settled on a standard frame proportion of four units horizontal to three units vertical. This 4:3 (1.33:1) aspect ratio was adopted for the dimensions of television

**Table 4.1** MPEG and video formats for DVD.

|  | **NTSC** | **PAL** |
|---|---|---|
| Compression format | MPEG-1 & MPEG-2 (CBR & VBR) | MPEG-1 & MPEG-2 (CBR & VBR) |
| Picture resolution | 704 × 480<br>352 × 480<br>352 × 240<br>352 × 576 | 720 × 480<br>704 × 576<br>720 × 576<br>352 × 288 |
| Pictures in group of pictures (GOP) | Fewer than 36 fields | Fewer than 30 fields |
| Aspect ratio | 4:3 or 16:9 | 4:3 or 16:9 |
| Bit-rate (maximum for audio, video and subpicture) | 9.8 Mbps | 9.8 Mbps |

screens by broadcasters in the late 1940s. The 1950s saw the advent of cinemascope and other 'widescreen' movie formats with aspect ratios of 1.85:1 or 2.35:1, but conventional television sets have retained the 1.33:1 aspect ratio to this day.

Traditionally, most widescreen movies have been adapted for display on TV using a pan/scan process. In pan/scan, a 1.33:1 viewing area is moved around over the original widescreen image in an attempt to follow the most important action in the frame, while material on either side of this area gets left out. Many viewers prefer the letterbox approach, in which a widescreen image is shown in full on a 1.33:1 screen, with black borders along the top and bottom.

When DVD-Video was defined, an effort was made to support display of widescreen movies by adopting the 16:9 (1.78:1) aspect ratio used in the digital television (DTV) format. This is not an aspect ratio actually used in film, but it is a close compromise for the common 1.85:1 film aspect ratio.

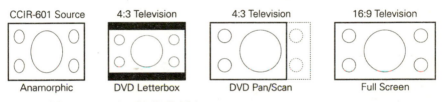

| CCIR-601 Source | 4:3 Television | 4:3 Television | 16:9 Television |
|---|---|---|---|
| Anamorphic | DVD Letterbox | DVD Pan/Scan | Full Screen |

**Figure 4.3** Aspect ratios for DVD-Video.

With 16:9, widescreen films are converted to an anamorphic video source, meaning that the picture is horizontally squeezed to fit into a 4:3 frame. Once encoded onto a DVD, the playback mode selected on the player determines how the anamorphic material is displayed. For a full-screen image, the viewer needs a wide-screen TV. With a standard TV, the user may select between viewing the horizontally-squeezed image as is (everything looks tall and narrow), letterboxed, or pan/scan. For the player to correctly pan/scan an anamorphic image, the pan/scan vectors must be encoded into the MPEG-2 data stream.

## Angles

One unique aspect of the DVD-Video format is its multi-angle feature. A single video stream may incorporate up to nine parallel video programs, and the viewer can, with a single click, switch between these angles without any

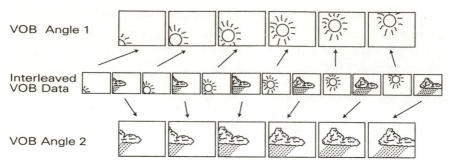

**Figure 4.4** The interleaving of multiple video angles in a single video stream (VOB).

break in video or audio continuity. This feature can provide multiple points-of-view for sporting events, music videos, and movies. The video quality of each angle is maintained because the maximum bit-rate of each of the video streams need drop only slightly to accommodate the data interleaving required.

# Audio on DVD-Video

## Basic and optional formats

While video provided the impetus for DVD's development, the format's designers understood that high-quality, multi-channel audio would be an essential ingredient for success, differentiating DVD from all other video formats. No other media allows for switching between languages on-the-fly, or enables such a broad range of audio formats.

DVD-Video supports two main digital audio formats: Linear PCM (similar to a CD) is uncompressed, while Dolby Digital (AC-3) is compressed to reduce bit-rate requirements. Either of these formats may potentially be

**Table 4.2** Audio formats for DVD-Video.

|  | **PCM** | **Dolby Digital** | **MPEG-1** | **MPEG-2** |
|---|---|---|---|---|
| Max. bit-rate | 6.144 Mbps | 448 kbps | 384 kbps | 912 kbps |
| Frequency | 48/96 kHz | 48 kHz | 48 kHz | 48 kHz |
| Max. channels | 4/8* | 6 | 2 | 8 |

* Up to eight channels of 48 kHz; up to four channels of 96 kHz.

used to deliver audio in both stereo and surround sound. Additional formats which may optionally be used for stereo or surround sound are MPEG, DTS (Digital Theatre Systems) or SDDS (Sony Dynamic Digital Sound).

## Multiple audio tracks

Just as DVD-Video's multi-angle feature allows seamless switching between multiple streams of MPEG video, the format supports seamless switching between multiple audio soundtracks for each video program. The specification allows the inclusion of up to eight independent mono, stereo or surround sound audio streams for every video track. Each of these soundtrack streams may be stored in any of DVD-Video's available audio formats.

DVD-Video's multiple audio streams may be used for different language versions of a soundtrack, different mixes, or commentary tracks by the director, actors, or special effects crew. They may also be used to deliver the soundtrack in different audio formats. To date, the most common use of this feature in consumer video titles has been to allow a preparation of a single disc for multiple language markets (e.g. English, French and Spanish tracks for North American release). The viewer switches between the audio tracks with the DVD remote control.

## Extensive PCM digital audio support

DVD-Video supports an extensive set of linear PCM multi-channel formats at 48 and 96 kHz sample rates, with word lengths ranging from 16 up to 24 bits (significantly greater resolution than the conventional CD). Total audio

**Table 4.3** PCM audio configurations in DVD-Video.

| Sample Rate (kHz) | Sample Word (bits) | Channels | | | | | | | |
|:---:|:---:|:---:|:---:|:---:|:---:|:---:|:---:|:---:|:---:|
| | | 1 | 2 | 3 | 4 | 5 | 6 | 7 | 8 |
| 48 | 16 | ☐ | ☐ | ☐ | ☐ | ☐ | ☐ | ☐ | ☐ |
| 48 | 20 | ☐ | ☐ | ☐ | ☐ | ☐ | ☐ | | |
| 48 | 24 | ☐ | ☐ | ☐ | ☐ | ☐ | | | |
| 96 | 16 | ☐ | ☐ | ☐ | ☐ | | | | |
| 96 | 20 | ☐ | ☐ | ☐ | | | | | |
| 96 | 24 | ☐ | ☐ | | | | | | |

bandwidth in the DVD-Video specification is limited to 6.144 Mbps. This imposes restrictions on the number of channels supported at the various sample rates and word lengths.

Even though the DVD-Video format supports multi-channel, high-resolution PCM audio, players are not required to reproduce this audio at full resolution, and the majority of DVD-Video players on the market provide only two discrete audio outputs. Additionally, most DVD-Video players decimate 96 kHz audio to 48 kHz prior to D/A conversion, and some players also truncate 20- and 24-bit samples to 16 bits. This means that while it is possible to create a DVD-Video soundtrack with high-resolution audio – including discrete multi-channel surround sound – it is not possible to guarantee that the viewer will hear the sound at full resolution. (Support for high-resolution audio *is* required for players in the DVD-Audio format).

Another factor influencing the choice of audio format is the fact that any data bandwidth allocated to audio is not available for video. With that in mind, many DVD title publishers choose to devote the bulk of the available bit-rate to achieving the best possible video encoding, while using Dolby Digital audio tracks (which require less bandwidth) rather than PCM.

# Still images and overlays

In order to deliver high-quality still images, as well as enable the menus that are used to navigate a DVD-Video title, the specification allows single frames of video to be encoded in full-colour and full-resolution. Although primarily used for menu backgrounds, still images may also be used for still shows and slide shows. A still show is a sequence of video images that can be advanced manually by the user, while a slide show is pre-programed to advance automatically. In both cases, still images may be accompanied by audio in any of the available audio formats.

## Subtitles and subpictures

When the entertainment industry defined their goals for DVD, they wanted support for subtitling in multiple languages, allowing a single version of a title to be released in several countries. As a result, the DVD-Video specification allows a given video stream to be accompanied by up to 32 subtitle streams. DVD-Video subtitles are subpicture overlays – images which are generated by the DVD player during playback and appear on top of background video or still images.

**Figure 4.5** A menu screen with a still graphic background.

**Figure 4.6** One use of subpicture overlays in DVD-Video is for subtitles.

Subpictures are not limited to subtitles. They may be used for other text information, such as instructions or karaoke lyrics, or for graphics such as buttons, highlights and animations. Subpicture overlays may be changed on a frame-by-frame basis and may fade in or fade out, wipe in colour or transparency, or scroll up and down the screen.

Any bitmap graphic up to 720 × 480 (NTSC) or 720 × 576 (PAL) may be used for a subpicture overlay. Colour depth is limited, however, to only four single-bit colour layers per frame, including the colour used for the background layer. Each layer may appear at its own transparency level, from transparent to opaque. The colours used on any given frame are drawn from a 16-colour palette that is pre-assigned to each Program Chain (more on Program Chains later).

# Additional features

## *Parental control*

DVD is the first video format that can actively modify playback based on the rating of the disc's content. Using mechanisms that also enable the format to switch between a director's cut of a movie and the theatrical release version, the DVD-Video format allows a rating to be assigned to a particular movie clip on a title. It also allows the viewer to set the movie rating level of the player.

When a disc is placed into a player, the rating level of the movie is mapped against the rating level set in the player. A player set to play only PG movies will automatically switch to a PG version of the movie, if one is included. But if the disc includes only an R-rated version, the player will refuse to play it.

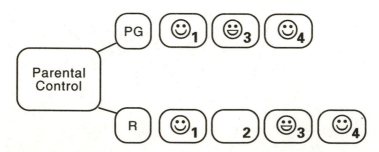

**Figure 4.7** With the parental control feature, a single DVD-Video can take different playback paths depending on the player setting and movie rating.

## Copy protection

One of the entertainment industry's most important requirements for DVD was copy protection. With both VHS piracy and CD bootlegging threatening worldwide entertainment media sales, major movie studios were unwilling to release near-master quality video and audio on a digital format that could be easily copied with no generation loss.

With the contribution of the cross-industry Copy Protection Technical Working Group (CPTWG), several methods of asset protection, both analog and digital, were included in the DVD format. Macrovision is used to prevent copying of the high-quality analog video output from the DVD player onto a VHS deck, and the CSS (Content Scrambling System) encryption scheme is used to scramble the digital data streams. Encrypted data can only be decrypted with a hardware chip in the DVD player or through specially-designed software for PC-based DVD decoding.

## Regional coding

The movie industry often releases theatrical films and home videos on different dates in different areas of the world. This may be with the aim of holding the video in a local market until after a film's theatrical release, or to allow time for the feature to be re-edited or dubbed into a new language for the target country.

To ensure that entertainment companies have control over the international distribution and timing of their DVD title releases, the DVD specification divides the world into six regions, as shown in Figure 4.8.

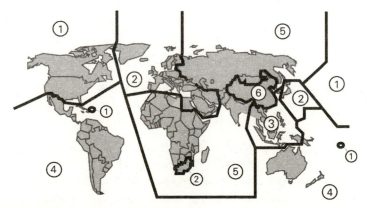

**Figure 4.8** Worldwide regions for regional coding.

Each DVD player is hardware-coded for a single region. At the discretion of the publisher, any given DVD-Video title may be coded during authoring to allow playback in one or more regions. For a regionally-coded DVD disc to play back, the regions of the title and the player must match. For example, DVD titles encoded as Region 2 for Japan will not play back in US players, which will only play discs encoded for Region 1. Titles may optionally be enabled for all regions.

# The structure of DVD-Video

To ensure consistent playback of DVD-Video discs on different players, the specification defines in detail the organization of a disc's content. This organization covers two inter-related aspects of DVD playback: the program material itself, and the logic determining the order and conditions of playback.

We have seen in the previous section that video, audio, graphics and subpictures are the main ingredients of a DVD-Video title, and that they need to be in certain supported formats to be included on a DVD-Video disc. We will see later how these elemental assets are eventually combined into a single multiplexed stream. These streams containing the material to be played back – the DVD's presentation data – are referred to as Video Objects (VOB), and are stored in containers called Video Object Sets (VOBS).

The question of which object plays back, and when, is determined by a set of instructions referred to as Program Chains (PGCs), which are organized into the navigational structures, called domains, that make up the logical structure of a DVD-Video title.

## Volumes and zones

The top level of organization on a DVD disc is a volume. A single-sided DVD (DVD-5 or DVD-9) contains a single DVD volume, while a double sided disc (DVD-10 or DVD-18) is made up of two separate volumes.

On a DVD-Video, the volume is made up of the UDF file system, a single DVD-Video zone, and a DVD-Others zone. The video zone contains all of the data elements for the set-top video title, while the DVD-Others zone is for any non-DVD-Video data, such as desktop computer applications.

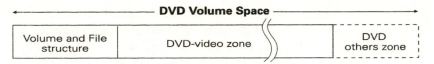

**Figure 4.9** The volume structure of a DVD-Video title.

The first part of the DVD-Video zone is the Video Manager (VMG) – a master directory for the data elements on the disc. The Video Manager is followed by up to 99 Video Title Sets, which include the video, audio and graphical elements of each title on the disc.

The Video Manager usually contains an introductory clip of video and audio, such as an opening logo, and a title menu that allows for navigation to the Video Title Sets. When the TITLE key on a DVD remote control is pressed, it will take the user back to this TITLE menu.

## Video Title Sets and Video Objects

The Video Title Sets that follow the Video Manager normally comprise the bulk of a DVD disc. A Video Title Set (VTS) is made up of a VTS Menu (VTSM) and one or more Video Titles (VTT). While a Title Set on early feature film DVDs usually contained just one Video Title (for the movie itself), it is not uncommon today for a release to include multiple Titles, including such added-value materials as interviews or behind-the-scenes

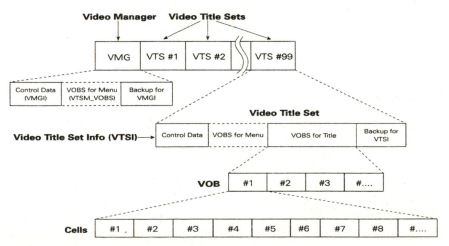

**Figure 4.10** The structure of a DVD-Video zone.

documentaries. Titles, in turn, may be broken down into Part of Titles (PTT) – akin to chapters in LaserDisc – which are commonly used to allow direct access to individual scenes.

The use of Title Sets enables DVD developers to allow viewers to jump directly to a menu for the current section (VTS) of the content without going back through the main menu for the disc. The MENU button on the player remote control is included for this function. Additionally, since all the video in a given VTS must be in the same aspect ratio, discs including video in both standard and widescreen ratios use multiple Title Sets.

The presentation data referenced by a Video Title is contained in a Video Object Set (VOBS), which is made up in turn of one or more Video Objects (VOB). A Video Object includes the video, audio, subpictures, and navigation data for a program. The VOB can be thought of as the basic media file of the DVD-Video disc. VOB files containing video and audio data can be played back individually on most desktop computers with DVD capability.

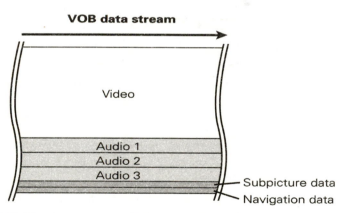

**Figure 4.11** The data stream of a DVD-Video VOB file.

Each VOB can be broken down into one or more Cells. The Cell is the lowest branch of the DVD data structure. A cell may be as large as an entire movie or as small as an MPEG GOP (Group of Pictures; more on this later). A Cell is the smallest unit that may be addressed directly when navigating during branching or other interactivity.

## Title organization

To illustrate how the structure of DVD-Video works in the real world, let us compare the organization of two different hypothetical titles. A simple feature film DVD with nine chapters, for instance, would have one Video Manager (incorporating the main menu), one Video Title Set, one Title, one VOBS made up of one VOB, and nine Cells.

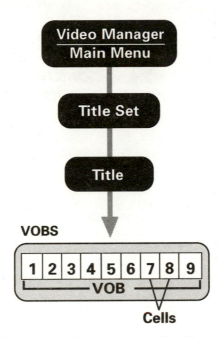

**Figure 4.12** The logical structure of a simple movie title with one menu and one program (a single VOBS containing a single VOB).

A highly elaborate music video title, on the other hand, might showcase fifteen artists, each with five music videos, a biography, and a slide show containing album covers with background music. In this case the disc might still have one Video Manager (with the main menu for the entire disc), but there would be fifteen Video Title Sets, one for each artist. Each VTS could include a menu (VTSM) for the content in that section, as well as the content itself, which would be seven Titles (five music videos, the artist's biography and a still show), each playing a VOB made up of one or more Cells.

The more complex example illustrates the reason why the DVD remote control has both TITLE and MENU keys. To return to the main menu for the entire DVD, the viewer would press the TITLE key. The main menu allows the viewer to choose from among the disc's Title Sets, which in this example means selecting the artist whose videos they want to see. Within a given

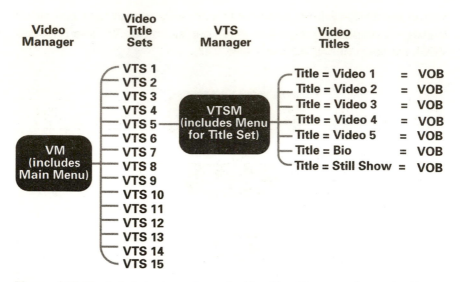

**Figure 4.13** The logical structure of a music video title with many artists, each with several video clips, a biography and a still show.

artist's Title Set, pressing the MENU key would take the viewer to the menu of Titles (the videos, biography and slide show) available in that particular Title Set.

## Program Chains

As we have learned, VOBs are the basic unit of media in DVD-Video, representing multiplexed audio, video, and subpicture assets. Program Chains (PGC), on the other hand, are the basic logical unit, a set of instructions telling the DVD player which VOBs should be played, under which conditions, and in what order. A DVD-Video title is essentially a collection of Program Chains and the VOB files to which those PGCs refer.

Each Program Chain is made up of a pre-command, a group of programs, and a post-command. The pre-command sets the condition for the VOBs that follow, such as which audio stream will be played, or whether a program has recently been viewed.

The pre-command is followed by a list of Cells to be played back from the referenced VOB. The list of Cells is similar to an Edit Decision List (EDL) in a nonlinear editing system. Two different programs (R-rated and PG-rated versions of a movie, for instance) may reference the same VOBs, but include different subsets of Cells. In the example in Figure 4.14, both Program Chains are playing back from the same stream. However, PGC-1 shows a video clip with rain and lightning, while PGC-2 shows only rain.

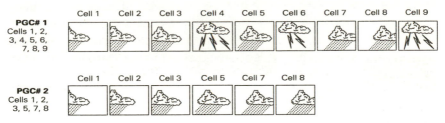

**Figure 4.14** Two Program Chains that take different paths through the same VOB.

After the series of listed Cells has been played, there follows a post-command. Post-commands are commonly used for tasks such as linking directly to another Program Chain, or returning to a main menu.

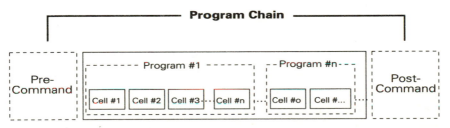

**Figure 4.15** The structure of a DVD-Video Program Chain.

## Navigation commands

In all, the DVD-Video specification offers a set of 128 possible navigation commands for use in Program Chains. These commands are broken down into a few basic categories: Jump and Link, Calculation, Comparison, Parameter Setting, and Program Flow. The use and combination of these commands allows for complex functions, such as keeping score in a game, controlling the navigation of a title, or ensuring that a unique ending is chosen for a movie.

Multiple commands are grouped together by using dummy PGCs, which are used only for their pre- and post-command areas and do not reference any VOBs. Dummy PGCs may also be used to move between Video Title Sets.

# Menus and interactivity

By now it should be evident that Program Chains allow the design of DVD-Video titles which are highly interactive. Whether the application is an interactive game or a movie with multiple story lines, DVD-Video has been structured to support a variety of complex responses to user interaction, offering control and flexibility that are unprecedented in a video format. This support ranges from DVD-Video's menu structure to its use of memory parameters.

## *Menu-based navigation*

As a descendant of the Video-CD format, DVD has inherited much of that format's support for hierarchical branching menus. This style of interactivity allows a viewer to navigate through a disc by jumping from menu to menu. Most DVD-Video movie releases support this basic approach, in which the viewer chooses playback parameters (the language of a subtitle track, for instance), jumps to various chapter points in the movie, or links to added features such as cast biographies, story boards, etc.

Menus are comprised of a background image (motion or still), a subpicture overlay, a button highlight area, and (sometimes) audio. If the DVD is set up to play in 16:9 aspect ratio, a different set of buttons and highlights must be created for each of three possible display modes: wide screen, letterbox, and pan/scan.

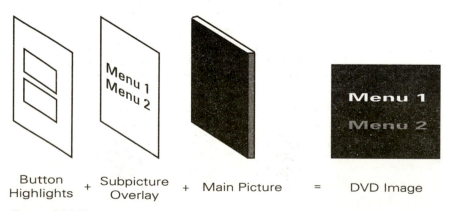

| Button Highlights | + | Subpicture Overlay | + | Main Picture | = | DVD Image |

**Figure 4.16** The composition of a DVD menu.

## *Buttons and highlights*

DVD-Video supports a variety of approaches to menu design. A background image may be either a motion video or a 24-bit colour still. Menu choices may be displayed in full colour as part of a background still, or as overlays using colours from the current subpicture palette.

As the viewer toggles through the menu with the arrow keys on the remote control, visual feedback indicates which menu item is currently selected. Feedback is also given when the viewer presses the ENTER key to activate a selection.

The most common approach to visual feedback is to use subpicture overlays. As we learned earlier in our discussion about subtitles, only four single-bit colours (each ranging from transparent to opaque) are available for overlays in a given frame (the colours are drawn from the 16-colour subpicture palette that is pre-assigned to each Program Chain). However, while the highlight colours are limited, this method offers the fastest navigation during playback. This is because the DVD player itself generates the overlay, which takes less time than reading and decompressing an image stored on the disc.

Another method of giving visual feedback is to create a series of linked menus, with different stored background images used to indicate a highlighted state for each menu choice. However, while this approach allows full colour-depth for the highlight graphics, it is more complex to implement, and slower during playback.

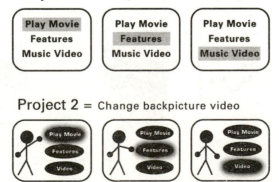

**Figure 4.17** Two methods of giving visual feedback to viewers on menu screens, one using subpicture overlays for highlights, the other using multiple backgrounds.

Whether visual feedback is provided on the background or by an overlay, the rectangular region of the screen that is reserved for each menu choice is defined as a button highlight. A button highlight may have an assigned colour and transparency for normal, selected, and activated states. (When visual feedback is provided strictly by background graphics, the button highlights are fully transparent.) A highlight colour may also be keyed over a predetermined colour in a background image or subpicture within the region. For example, a text selection may be in black, but when it is selected, the letters turn green. This allows the highlighting of complex shapes, even though the highlight region is defined as a rectangular box.

## System menus

The DVD specification defines a certain number of menus available to the user through the press of a button on the remote control. These are known as system menus and are defined as: Title, Root, Part-of-Title, Audio, Angle, and Subpicture.

The Title menu resides in the Video Manager and is used to access Title Sets on the disc. It may be accessed with the TITLE key on the remote control.

The Root menu resides within each Video Title Set, and may be accessed with the MENU key.

Audio, Angle, and Subpicture menus reside within each VTS, and may be used to change the current audio track (e.g. PCM or Dolby Digital 5.1), video angle (e.g. wide or close-up), and subpicture stream (e.g. English, Spanish or French).

Whenever a system menu is accessed by pressing the MENU's key on the remote control, the DVD player stores its current playback location. When finished with the menu, the viewer need only press the same key a second time to return to that same location. This allows the viewer to pause movie playback, make an adjustment to playback conditions (change audio format or subtitle language, for instance) and then resume watching in the exact same place.

Although the specification designates areas for MENUS in the Video Manager and Video Title Set, all of the interactivity, subpictures, and highlights available on menus are also available within the course of VOB playback. Placing menus in the Video Manager and Video Title Set allows the viewer quickly to jump to them using the remote control. Beyond that

**Figure 4.18** A typical Title menu (main menu) offers access to the main feature, extra content and set-up screens.

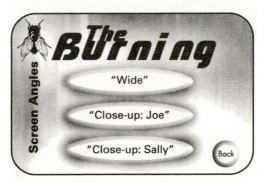

**Figure 4.19** A typical Root menu offers access to the contents of a given Video Title Set.

**Figure 4.20** Audio, Angle, and Subpicture menus allow the viewer to choose among different playback options for the current program.

important distinction, however, the difference between a movie and a menu is largely a useful concept for title design rather than an actual functional limitation.

## Complex interactivity

Understanding that a movie may incorporate the full range of menu functionality opens up rich new possibilities in DVD-Video title design. For example, a movie may be playing back when a subpicture appears, indicating a choice for the viewer to make in the direction of the story. Pressing the left or right keys on the remote would highlight the choices, while pressing ENTER would link the viewer to a new Program Chain. This type of in-play menu may be associated with a specific time in the program, with the choices continually changing as the movie plays. To speed the interactivity, selections may be made to auto-activate so that the user does not have to hit an ENTER key.

**Figure 4.21** Interactive titles such as games may use on-screen buttons allowing the user to make in-play choices that direct the course of the action.

Titles involving extensive user interaction during the course of a disc's play represent a new genre of home video entertainment. Such titles might include interactive movies in which the viewer chooses the outcome of each scene, or where the path of the story is determined by decisions made earlier in the program.

## System parameters and General parameters

To fully realize the interactive potential of DVD-Video, the specification requires that players support two kinds of memory parameters: System and General. System parameters are used by the DVD player to remember default settings such as language, aspect ratio, and Parental Rating level. These parameters may be set either by the viewer or by a DVD title as it plays.

General parameters (GPRMs), on the other hand, can only be addressed by the DVD disc in play. Sixteen 16-bit memory locations are available to be used for basic computation or storing values. GPRMs may be used to keep track of the number of lives a viewer has left in a game, for instance, or to remember which segments of an interactive story have already been viewed.

## Title examples

As explained earlier, the DVD-Video format's flexibility allows a wide range of possibilities for title design. The following example shows a simple DVD title with a Title menu, a PTT (Chapter) menu branching to multiple chapter points, a Language menu stemming to an Audio menu and a Subtitle menu, and a still image for the actors' biographies. Many Hollywood-style DVD movies are using a basic template along these lines.

An example of a slightly more complex title would be a DVD of music videos featuring different artists. In the template below, the title begins with a Title menu which branches into a list of titles, an Audio menu, and a

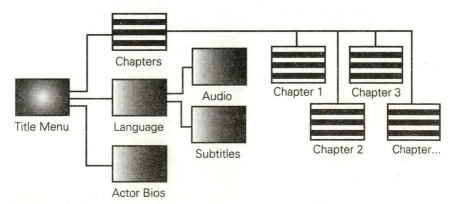

**Figure 4.22** Example flowchart for a basic feature-film title on DVD-Video.

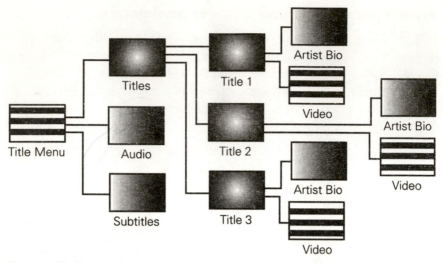

**Figure 4.23** Example flowchart for a music video release on DVD-Video.

Subtitle menu. The menu listing each Title is used to branch to individual Title Sets (VTS), one for each artist. Within each VTS, there is a choice between a video and an artist biography. In this layout, a viewer would use the TITLE key to return to a list of all the artists on the disc, while the MENU key would be used to display the choice of materials for the current artist.

DVD titles can quickly become quite complex. Once motion video menus are included, General parameters are used, and multiple story-lines are devised, the template for a highly-interactive title may be challenging to visualize or to represent graphically. Applications for such titles might include interactive training manuals, multilanguage education, archival video and audio storage, interactive movies, games, and DVD-Video/DVD-ROM hybrids with databases and Web connectivity.

# Chapter 5

# DVD-Audio: fidelity and flexibility

We have seen from the foregoing chapter that the DVD-Video specification defines a rich and versatile format that takes home video far beyond its previous boundaries. One thing that DVD-Video was not intended to do, however, was to replace CD-Audio as the primary carrier of prerecorded music for the record industry. While the home video and record industries are similar in many respects, each business has its own unique requirements for distribution media.

Like DVD-Video, DVD-Audio is built on the foundation of DVD-ROM. So a DVD-Audio disc is actually a DVD-ROM disc that includes a zone of material supported by the DVD-Audio specification (and may optionally contain a zone of DVD-Video material as well). These zones are essentially directories or folders within the UDF file system.

The DVD-Audio specification incorporates many of the same DVD-Video navigational and architectural features discussed in the previous chapter, but it also includes several new features devised specifically for audio-based multimedia. Additionally, it supports even higher audio fidelity and more flexible multichannel playback options. Thus, while the two formats are closely related, DVD-Audio extends DVD-Video to create a truly distinct product tailored for audio-centric applications. For those intending to create DVD-Audio titles, this chapter will clarify the functional and technical similarities and differences between the new DVD-Audio format and its established DVD-Video sibling.

# Design objectives

In developing the DVD-Audio format, the DVD Forum's Working Group-4 and the ISC began with a set of objectives. The most important of these are listed in Table 5.1.

**Table 5.1** Primary design objectives for DVD-Audio.

---

High quality audio – the new format should support the very highest quality audio possible.

Multichannel audio – the new format should permit extensive multichannel capabilities, and should recognize the fact that multichannel programs might be played back in venues where only stereo monitoring was available.

Additional data – text data, still images and video should be accommodated within the format.

Navigation – with DVD-Video now established, various interactivity features should be supported.

Simple interface – the new format should accommodate a simple CD player-like interface for playback settings, where elaborate controls and visual displays are impractical.

DVD-Video compatibility – the new format should be broadly compatible with DVD-Video and permit utilization of DVD-Video features, where appropriate.

Copyright – the format should support effective anti-copying and anti-piracy measures.

---

The list is varied, and in some cases the objectives might seem potentially at cross-purposes. The challenge confronting Working Group-4 was to create a flexible format which would serve multiple purposes in a variety of settings.

# DVD-Audio players

To ensure DVD-Audio's flexibility across a wide range of applications, Working Group-4 decided not to attempt to define one single set of features that would be mandated for all DVD-Audio players. Instead, a DVD-Audio disc may contain a variety of different content types, each of which will play back on one or more of several different player types designed for different playback settings.

While this approach sounds complicated, much of the distinction between the different envisioned playback settings boils down to the question of whether or not video display is available. With DVD-Video, it was reasonable to expect that video display would always be available at playback. However, with an audio format, it is crucial to support playback without a video display, particularly in such situations as a 'Walkman' style portable, a 'boom box,' or a car. Even for home listening, requiring video support in all players would increase manufacturing costs, making it harder to reach the less expensive end of the audio player market.

Although the need for video-less playback was clear, DVD-Audio's developers also needed to support all the visual extras that consumers would expect from a next-generation entertainment format: graphics, text and motion video. To cover all bases, Working Group-4 envisioned that five roughly-defined player types might possibly be used to play back content from a disc in DVD-Audio format. These include:

- A simple Audio-only player that has no video output, and navigates the disc linearly using a list of tracks that is analogous to the Table of Contents (TOC) on a CD.
- A smart Audio-only player (still no video output) that gives the user more choice of how to navigate the material on the disc, and may include an LCD display to show song titles and other text information such as lyrics.
- An Audio-with-Video player that supports navigational choice and includes video outputs to support multimedia, including visual menus, album artwork, 'slide show' graphics and motion video (such as music videos).
- A Universal player that offers the same audio and multimedia support as the Audio-with-Video DVD-Audio player, but also plays DVD-Video discs.
- A DVD-Video player, which might be used to play optional video content that has been included on a DVD-Audio disc (although the DVD-Audio content on a DVD-Audio disc will not play on a DVD-Video player).

Whilst the different player types may be inferred from the DVD-Audio specification, it is considered unlikely that all of them will actually reach the market. In particular, it is unclear what demand there might be for the Audio-with-Video player that is not a Universal player. Similarly, many observers believe that there will be little justification for a distinct Video-only player once the Universal player is available. Eventually, then, new consumer DVD players may well be sold in just two main categories: Audio-only and Universal.

One way to easily visualize the difference between the two main categories of DVD-Audio players (Audio-only and Universal) is to compare the prototypical remote control implied for each type in the specification. The Universal player's remote control looks very much like that of a DVD-Video player:

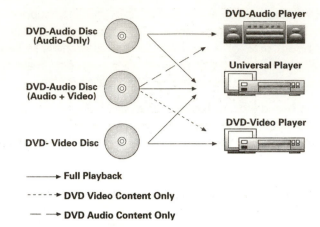

──────▶ **Full Playback**

- - - - -▶ **DVD Video Content Only**

— —▶ **DVD Audio Content Only**

**Figure 5.1** DVD-Audio disc and player types.

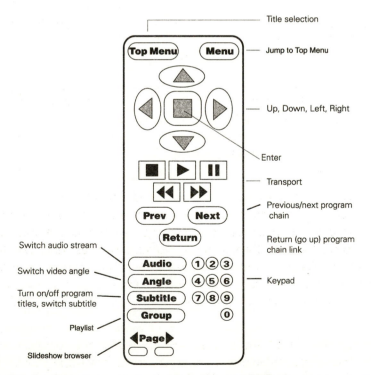

**Figure 5.2** Example of a remote control for a Universal DVD player.

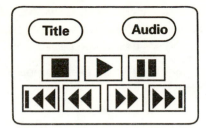

**Figure 5.3** Example of a remote control for an Audio-only DVD-Audio player.

In contrast, the minimal set of functions required to control the Audio-only player makes for a very simple remote control indeed (see Figure 5.3).

# DVD-Audio content

While the availability of different player types allows DVD-Audio discs to be played in a variety of settings, it also means that it is possible for a DVD-Audio disc to include some types of content that will not be available for playback in some situations. By choosing which types of content are put on a given DVD-Audio title, it is the producer who decides what the end-user's experience will be in various playback settings.

The base-case DVD-Audio disc is one that contains no graphics, text or motion video information. This 'Pure Audio' disc supports higher fidelity, greater capacity and more channels than a CD, but it functions in much the same way, with similar track-based navigation. Pure Audio discs play on both Audio-only and Universal DVD-Audio players, but they do not play on DVD-Video players.

Somewhat more sophisticated DVD-Audio titles may be created by adding text that accompanies the music (lyrics, for example), or using the format's logical structure to offer listeners different navigational options, such as multiple paths (playlists) through the audio material. These discs will still play on the simple Audio-only players, but their more sophisticated features will come to life when they are played on smart Audio-only players, or on video-enabled players such as Universal players. They do not play on DVD-Video players.

More complex DVD-Audio titles will take greater advantage of the format's multimedia capabilities, using visual menus for navigation, slide shows with audio, and motion video. Once again, these titles will play audio on

Audio-only players, but without all the extras that will be viewable on video-enabled players such as Universal players. If such a disc includes motion video content, that content (only) will typically be playable on DVD-Video players.

Table 5.2 provides an overview of some common combinations of disc contents and player types.

**Table 5.2** Disc contents and player types.

| Player type | Disc/Contents | | |
|---|---|---|---|
| | DVD-Audio disc without video | DVD-Audio disc with video | DVD-Video disc |
| Audio-only DVD-audio player | • Audio<br>• Text information | • Audio elements of DVD-Audio and DVD-Video titles | Not playable |
| Universal DVD-Audio player | • Audio<br>• Still pictures<br>• Text information | • Visual menus<br>• All audio, text, graphic and video content | • All DVD-Video content supported |
| DVD-Video player | Not playable | • Video content only | • All DVD-Video content supported |

# Audio formats

The core content type of the DVD-Audio format is, obviously, audio. While the DVD-Video specification gives equal weight to both linear PCM (pulse code modulation) and compressed audio formats such as Dolby Digital (AC-3), the DVD-Audio specification puts the priority on delivering the highest possible audio fidelity, and thus focuses primarily on PCM.

PCM data may be stored in either of two forms: linear (LPCM) or 'packed' using Meridian Lossless Packing (MLP). All players are required to support both LPCM and MLP audio in either stereo or multi-channel configurations. Players with video outs must also support Dolby Digital. Optional audio formats such as DTS or others not yet defined may be supported at the manufacturer's discretion.

A DVD-Audio disc may offer up to two audio streams in any given program. The first stream is required to be PCM (stereo or multichannel), the second stream (if any) may be in an optional audio format.

## *Audio resolution*

Within the PCM approach (LPCM or MLP), DVD-Audio offers content developers a wide array of choices regarding resolution. In PCM, the resolution of a given audio stream depends on two factors: the word-length and the sample-rate. The sample-rate is the number of times per second that the amplitude of the source analog waveform is sampled for conversion into a digitally stored value. The word-length is the number of bits available to store the value of each sample.

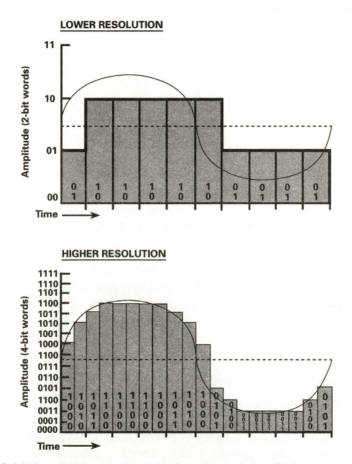

**Figure 5.4** When digitizing an analog waveform, the resolution (fidelity to the input signal) may be improved by increasing the sample-rate (number of samples per unit of time), the word-length (number of bits per sample), or both.

DVD-Audio's PCM support covers two families of sample-rates. One family is based on the 44.1 kHz rate of the audio CD, and also includes the multiples 88.2 and 176.4 kHz. The other family starts with the 48 kHz rate commonly used for audio in video formats, and adds 96 and 192 kHz.

**Table 5.3** Sample-rate families in DVD-Audio.

|                     | 44.1 kHz family | | | 48 kHz family | | |
| ------------------- | -------- | --------- | ---------- | ------- | ------- | -------- |
| **Sample-rate**     | 44.1 kHz | 88.2 kHz  | 176.4 kHz  | 48 kHz  | 96 kHz  | 192 kHz  |
| **Maximum Channels**| 6        | 6         | 2          | 6       | 6       | 2        |

DVD-Audio also includes support for several word-lengths, including not only the 16-bit samples used in CD-Audio, but also 20- and 24-bit samples. A longer word-length translates into finer resolution and a wider dynamic range.

## Multichannel sound

Of all of DVD-Audio's features, the one that consumers are generally expected to find most appealing is the format's ability to deliver multichannel sound. In each sample-rate family, the highest sample-rate (176.4 or 192.0 kHz) is supported only for mono or two-channel playback. The rest of the rates (44.1, 48, 88.2, and 96 kHz) are supported for mono up through six channels.

DVD-Audio's maximum data-rate allocable to audio – 9.6 Mbps – places limits on the total data bandwidth available to spread amongst the channels. Six channels of 20-bit audio at either 88.2 or 96 kHz, for instance, would substantially exceed the format's data-rate. The specification offers two complementary strategies for dealing with this limitation. One is MLP (explained below), the other is mixed resolutions.

Mixed resolutions allow the producer to prioritize the allocation of bits amongst the channels in a given audio track. Each channel is assigned to one of two Channel Groups, with the resolution of Group 1 always equal to or better than that of Group 2. Within a given track, the sample-rates used for all the channels in both groups must be from the same family.

Assignment of channels to groups, and selection of attributes within each group, may be changed on a track-by-track basis. To regulate the use of mixed resolutions amongst channels, most – but not all – of the reasonably foreseeable possibilities for varying the resolution of up to six channels are defined in the format's 21 supported channel assignments.

**Table 5.4** Supported sample-rate and word-length combinations for DVD-Audio's two Channel Groups.

|  | **If Channel Group 1 is:** | **. . . then Channel Group 2 may be:** |
|---|---|---|
| Sample rate | 48 kHz | 48 kHz |
|  | 96 kHz | 96 or 48 kHz |
|  | <u>192 kHz*</u> | – |
|  | 44.1 kHz | 44.1 kHz |
|  | 88.2 kHz | 88.2 or 44.1 kHz |
|  | 176.4 kHz* | – |
| Word length | 16 bits | 16 bits |
|  | 20 bits | 20 or 16 bits |
|  | 24 bits | 24, 20 or 16 bits |

* When sample rate = 192 kHz or 176 kHz, number of channels must be two or less (2ch Stereo or monaural).

**Table 5.5** Supported channel assignments for DVD-Audio's two Channel Groups.

|  |  | **ch0** | **ch1** | **ch2** | **ch3** | **ch4** | **ch5** |
|---|---|---|---|---|---|---|---|
|  | 1 | C |  |  |  |  |  |
|  | 2 | L | R |  |  |  |  |
|  | 3 | L | R | S |  |  |  |
|  | 4 | L | R | Ls | Rs |  |  |
|  | 5 | L | R | Lfe |  |  |  |
| Priority to | 6 | L | R | Lfe | S |  |  |
| front | 7 | L | R | Lfe | Ls | Rs |  |
| L and R | 8 | L | R | C |  |  |  |
|  | 9 | L | R | C | S |  |  |
|  | 10 | L | R | C | Ls | Rs |  |
|  | 11 | L | R | C | Lfe |  |  |
|  | 12 | L | R | C | Lfe | S |  |
|  | 13 | L | R | C | Lfe | Ls | Rs |
|  | 14 | L | R | C | S |  |  |
| Priority to | 15 | L | R | C | Ls | Rs |  |
| front | 16 | L | R | C | Lfe |  |  |
| L, R and C | 17 | L | R | C | Lfe | S |  |
|  | 18 | L | R | C | Lfe | Ls | Rs |
| Priority to | 19 | L | R | Ls | Rs | Lfe |  |
| corners: | 20 | L | R | Ls | Rs | C |  |
| L, R, Ls, Rs | 21 | L | R | Ls | Rs | C | Lfe |
|  |  |  |  | **Channel Group 1** |  | **Channel Group 2** |  |

Key: C = centre; L = front left; R = front right; S = surround (mono); LS = left surround; Rs = right surround; Lfe = low frequency effects (subwoofer)

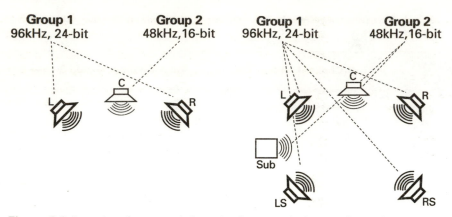

**Figure 5.5** Examples of supported channel assignments. Assignment 8 uses three channels, with priority to left and right. Assignment 21 uses six channels, with priority to the four corners (left and right front, left and right surround).

To illustrate the range of channel groupings permitted by the specification, a couple of examples are shown with possible attribute assignments in Figure 5.5.

## Playing time and lossless packing

Because DVD-Audio supports so many different variations of sample-rates, word-lengths and channel configurations, the capacity, in minutes, of the format may vary widely. The ability to vary these attributes on a track-by-track basis simply adds to the complexity of stating the maximum playing time. However, it is clear that the use of more channels, more samples, or more bits per sample will all result in shorter playback capacity.

**Table 5.6** Example playing times for different audio variations.

| Quantization (bits) | Sample-rate (kHz) | Channels | Data-rate (Mbps) | Time (minutes) |
|---|---|---|---|---|
| 16 | 44.1 | 2 | 1.41 | 422 |
| 16 | 48 | 2 | 1.54 | 388 |
| 20 | 96 | 4 | 7.68 | 78 |
| 24 | 192 | 2 | 9.22 | 65 |

Note: Single-layer, single-sided disc with no lossless compression; assumes 5 per cent overhead for navigation and formatting data.

As shown in the table, at the same resolution as CD-Audio (stereo 16-bit/44.1 kHz), DVD-Audio is capable of far greater playing time than CD-Audio's 74 minutes. But even with DVD-Audio's greater data rate and data capacity, full support for high-fidelity surround sound (six channels of 24-bit/96 kHz audio, for instance) would exceed the format's maximum bit-rate and quickly use up the available storage. To address this issue, Working Group-4 adopted the Meridian Lossless Packing (MLP) compression system developed by Meridian Audio and licensed through Dolby Laboratories. Because it is a completely lossless system, a decoded MLP datastream is bit-for-bit identical to the pre-encoded PCM source stream.

MLP permits substantial reduction in the bandwidth required to store high-quality multichannel PCM audio. The efficiency of the algorithm varies with the program content, particularly for material at sample-rates of 44.1 or 48 kHz. For higher sample-rates (88.2, 96, 176.4 and 192 kHz), however, MLP has been demonstrated reliably to achieve a 45 per cent reduction in bandwidth requirements. This allows a DVD-5 disc to be used for the presentation of up to 74 minutes of program using six channels of 24-bit/96 kHz audio. DVD-Audio discs are not required to use MLP, but decoding capability for MLP is mandated for all DVD-Audio players.

## SMART content and down-mixing

One of the problems confronted by Working Group-4 in defining DVD-Audio stems from the fact that, aside from home theatre systems, most playback situations (stereo receivers, headphones, and boom-boxes, for instance) are currently configured for stereo. To ensure that a DVD-Audio disc will always play, regardless of the available monitoring configuration, WG-4 had to define how a player should present multichannel programs in situations where only stereo playback is available. The difficulty is that a program mixed for surround presentation may not sound correctly balanced in stereo, particularly if the player simply ignores the surround channels.

DVD-Audio will allow both stereo and multichannel mixes of the same music to be delivered on one disc. So one solution would have been to require that every disc that includes a multichannel program must also include a two-channel version of the same program. However, that would have imposed significant limitations on the playing time of discs with multichannel programs.

Instead, WG-4 mandated that players support an approach championed by Warner Bros. Records called 'SMART Content' (System Managed Audio

**Table 5.7** Relying on the SMART Content feature to create a stereo down-mix in two-channel playback situations (Case A) allows a longer playing time compared to including a separate stereo mix (Case B).

**SMART Content vs Separate 2-channel Mix**

| | MULTICHANNEL MIX | | | | | | | | 2-CHANNEL MIX | | | | Total Bit Rate | | Playing Time 4.6 GB |
| | Group 1 Left Front, Centre, Right Front | | | | Group 2 Left Rear, Right Rear, Subwoofer | | | | | | | | | | |
| | Channels | Sample rate kHz | Bit depth | Mbit Rate/Sec | Channels | Sample Rate kHz | Bit Depth | Mbit Rate/Sec | Channels | Sample Rate kHz | Bit Depth | Mbit Rate/Sec | Mbit Rate/Sec | Mbytes/ Minutes | Minutes |
|---|---|---|---|---|---|---|---|---|---|---|---|---|---|---|---|
| **Case A** | 3 | 88.2 | 20 | 5.29 | 3 | 44.1 | 20 | 2.65 | SMART Content Down-mix | | | | 7.94 | 59.54 | 77.27 |
| **Case B** | 3 | 88.2 | 20 | 5.29 | 3 | 44.1 | 20 | 2.65 | No SMART Content | | | | 9.35 | 70.12 | 66.60 |
| | | | | | | | | | 2 | 44.1 | 16 | 1.41 | | | |

ResourceTechnique). SMART allows the producer to determine, in advance, a set of coefficients defining the relative level, panning and phase that will be applied to each channel of a multichannel mix if it is combined into stereo. A SMART down-mix will only be played if a discrete two-channel mix of a given program has not been included on the disc.

SMART coefficients are specified as 8-bit numbers in a six-by-two matrix, along with a phase bit for each channel. A set of sixteen tables of these coefficients may be defined for each Audio Object Set (more on these below). The table for each individual track of a Title may be selected from amongst these sixteen. This allows producers a workable means to control the sound of their music in cases where their multichannel mix is down-mixed by the player.

# Value-added content

While audio playback is at the heart of DVD-Audio, the format is also intended to offer a workable platform for the kinds of value-added multimedia features which have proven difficult to deliver to the mass market on formats such as CD-ROM and Enhanced CD. These features include graphical accompaniment for the music, text information about the music and the artist, and motion video such as music videos or interviews.

## Still pictures

The DVD-Audio specification fully supports the display of still pictures during audio playback, and offers the producer a wide range of options as to when and how the pictures are shown.

Still-graphics in DVD-Audio are MPEG-2 encoded images. The basic graphical unit is an ASV (Audio Still Video), composed of an MPEG still, a subpicture overlay (SPU), and highlight information (HLI). The subpicture and highlight layers are optional.

ASVs are grouped into sets of graphics referred to as ASVUs (Audio Still Video Units), each of which may contain up to 99 ASVs (individual images). While the data size of an individual ASV may vary greatly, typical ASVs may be expected to average about 100 KB.

The total size of an ASVU may not exceed 2 Megabytes, which is the size of the buffer that player manufacturers are required to provide to allow ASVUs to be preloaded into player memory. This preloading process

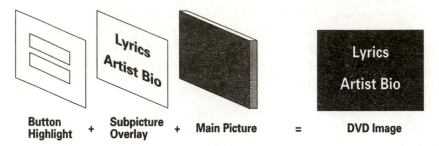

| Button Highlight | + | Subpicture Overlay | + | Main Picture | = | DVD Image |

**Figure 5.6** An ASV is composed of a main picture (MPEG still) plus optional subpicture overlay and highlights.

ensures that players will not interrupt audio playback in order to read graphical data from the disc. For instance, a listener can browse a series of still graphics without affecting the currently playing song.

The portion of audio over which the images from a given ASVU are intended to display is referred to as the ASVU range. An ASVU range may be either a single track or a set of tracks. From an authoring point of view, it is crucial to realize that audio output is muted during preloading of ASVUs. Depending on player design, the duration of this muting is likely to be at least two seconds, possibly more. Thus each ASVU range is separated by a silence of at least two seconds. This limitation will require careful planning of graphics usage in situations such as live albums, where audio programs may continue for long periods without the opportunity to load a new ASVU.

For each ASVU, the producer defines a playback mode that determines the order and duration of graphical display. Browseable graphics have a defined minimum and maximum on-screen duration, but allow the user to skip forward through the set of images by using the remote control. Slideshow graphics, on the other hand, are displayed for a predetermined amount of time.

Within each of these modes, the order in which the images is displayed may be defined as sequential (order predetermined by the producer), random, or shuffle (random, but no image repeated until every image has been shown). The format supports a variety of start and end effects (wipes and dissolves) as transitions between images.

The specification also allows the highlights within a given ASV to change over time. This is useful for content such as song lists, lyrics or libretto. Links allowing listeners to navigate to different parts of a song by clicking on lyrics are expected to be a common feature of DVD-Audio titles.

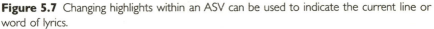

**Figure 5.7** Changing highlights within an ASV can be used to indicate the current line or word of lyrics.

## Text information

The DVD-Audio specification provides for storage of text information on disc, although inclusion of text is not mandatory. Text support is provided for multiple 'language units', with up to eight languages available on any given disc. Two character types are supported. For languages such as English that use single-byte characters (ISO8859-1), text is structured for presentation as 'pages' of four lines of up to 30 characters each. Japanese and other languages using double-byte characters (JIS Kanji) are organized into pages of two lines of up to 15 characters each.

The manner in which any given player uses this text information (if at all) is left to the discretion of the player manufacturer. A player with video output, for instance, may display the text on screen. But the size of the pages defined by the specification suggests that the primary application is envisioned as an LCD screen on 'smart' Audio-only players, Audio-with-Video players, and/or Universal players.

The specification defines two distinct types of text. Audio Text Data is intended for the display of static information that is not synchronized to the audio program. If Audio Text Data is used at all, it must include the Album title, 'Group' name (more about Groups later) and Track name. It may also include optional information such as the name(s) of the artist and composer. Up to 64 KB of data may be included for each language unit.

Real Time Text is stored on disc as part of the audio stream, and may be synchronized to audio playback. Ideal for lyrics and libretto, Real Time Text may also be used for context-dependent commentary such as running liner notes. Once again, the extent to which Real Time Text or Audio Text Data are supported by a given player is up to the hardware manufacturer.

### Video on DVD-Audio

DVD-Audio's support for motion video is substantially similar to that of DVD-Video, using Video Objects (VOBs) comprised of MPEG-2 video plus audio and optional subtitles. However, some advanced features that are supported in DVD-Video VOBs – such as parental control and complex interactivity – are not supported in all DVD-Audio settings. In order to understand these limitations fully, it is necessary to first understand the overall organization of the DVD-Audio format.

# The structure of DVD-Audio

As noted above, a DVD-Audio disc is a DVD-ROM disc that includes a special zone (the Audio_TS folder or directory) for DVD-Audio material. A DVD-Audio disc may also include a Video_TS folder for an optional DVD-Video zone, as well as a DVD-Others zone for applications and data (e.g. a browser for Web connectivity) that may be accessed from a computer-hosted DVD-ROM drive.

The overall volume structure of the DVD-Audio disc requires the DVD-Audio area to appear before the DVD-Video area and any other non-Audio/Video files and directories.

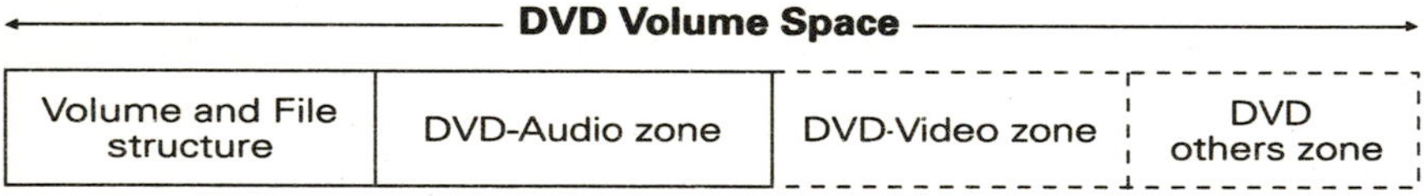

**Figure 5.8** The volume structure of a DVD-Audio disc.

As with DVD-Video, the final playback experience of a given DVD-Audio title involves two inter-related aspects of DVD playback: the program data itself (audio, still pictures, text and motion video) and the logic determining the order and conditions of playback. But because DVD-Audio discs are intended for playback on a number of different player types, the way in which the information on the disc is utilized and experienced also depends on the type of player.

## Multiple content managers

In the world of DVD, the first place a player goes to find out what content is present on a given disc is a directory referred to as a Manager. In our earlier discussion about the structure of DVD-Video, we learned about the Video Manager (VMG) in the DVD-Video zone. A DVD-Audio disc which includes an optional DVD-Video zone will naturally include a VMG as well, but this VMG is only used if the disc is played in a DVD-Video player. For playback in a DVD-Audio player, the specification requires inclusion in the audio zone of several different content directories, each used to accommodate a different playback situation (player).

The most basic form of Manager in DVD-Audio is the SAMG (Simple Audio Manager). Containing a list of up to 314 tracks, it serves the same function as the TOC (Table of Contents) on a CD-Audio disc. Simple Audio-only players look at SAMG to find the information they need for linear, track-based navigation of the disc.

As mentioned earlier, 'smart' Audio-only players, Audio-with-Video players and Universal players all support more sophisticated navigation than the simple Audio-only players. The directory information these players need is found in the AMG (Audio Manager). Smart Audio-only players use a section of AMG designated as AOTT, while Audio-with-Video players and Universal players use the AVTT section. Simple Audio-only players, meanwhile, ignore AMG completely.

## Data structure: Audio Object Sets and Audio Objects

Like the DVD-Video specification, the DVD-Audio specification describes two parallel organizational constructs: the data structure and the logical structure. When we discussed the organization of the DVD-Video zone on a DVD-Video disc, we learned that conceptually the zone is made up of navigational structures called domains, including a Video Manager (VMG) and one or more Video Title Sets (VTS). The presentation data referenced from within these domains is found in containers called Video Object Sets (VOBS) which contain Video Objects (VOBs).

Similarly, the DVD-Audio zone includes two domains: AMG (the Audio Manager described above) and Audio Title (ATT). The presentation data referenced from AMG (visual menus, if any) is contained in a VOBS. The presentation data referenced from ATT, meanwhile, is contained in one or more Audio Object Sets (AOBS).

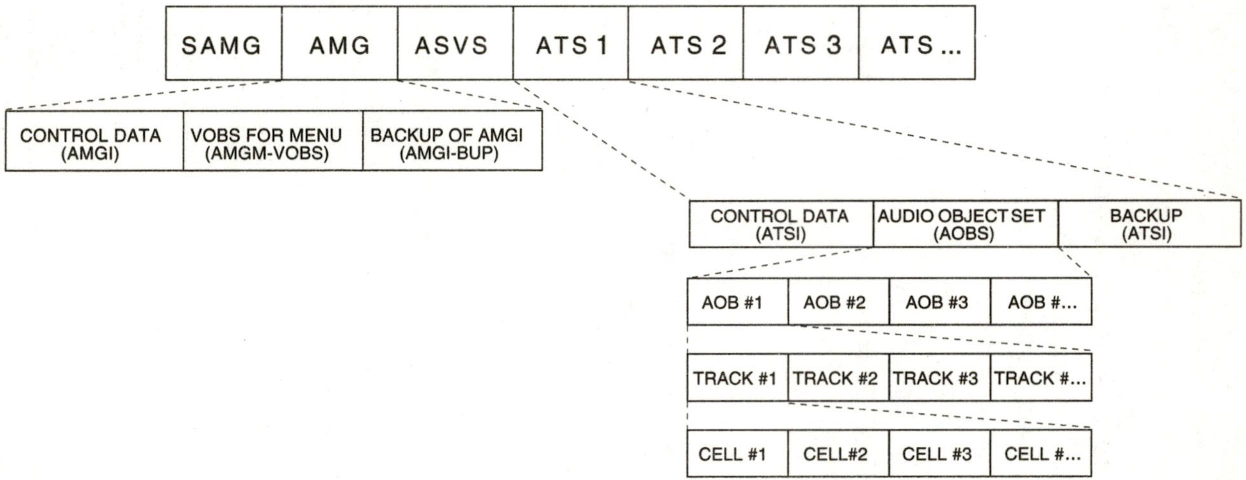


**Figure 5.9** The data structure of the DVD-Audio zone.

Each AOBS is comprised of some number of Audio Objects (AOBs). Analogous to VOBs, AOBs are made up of one or more Tracks (songs or compositions) of audio, optionally accompanied by the still images and/or Real Time Text discussed earlier. Tracks, in turn, are made up of one or more Cells.

## Logical structure: Albums, Groups and Tracks

DVD-Audio players which read AMG (all except simple Audio-only players) are able to take advantage of DVD-Audio's capacity to organize material hierarchically rather than simply linearly. This logical hierarchy exists in parallel to the format's data structure; it is based on five different levels: Album, Group, Title, Track and Index.

Each side of a DVD-Audio disc contains one Album. Each Album may contain up to nine Groups, each of which is essentially a playlist specifying the playback order of a number of Titles. While any Title may contain up to 99 Tracks, there may be no more than 99 Tracks total within a single Group.

As on a CD, a Track may be thought of as a single audio program (i.e. a song). Audio attributes such as channel assignment, sample-rate, and word-length may be changed on Track boundaries (players may mute during such attribute changes). An Index is a reference point to a portion of an audio Track (Cell), and there may be up to 99 Indices within a single Track.

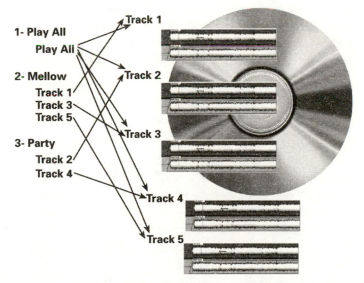

**Figure 5.10** A DVD-Audio Album with three Groups, one playing all Tracks, a second playing just mellow Tracks, and a third playing just party Tracks.

While this hierarchy has many levels, in practice the end-user is never aware of the existence of Titles. On a smart Audio-only player, for instance, a listener would normally be able to play any Track using the remote control by simply entering a Group number and then the number of a Track within that Group.

Because a Group is simply a playlist, a given Track may be referenced by more than one Group. On an album with twenty audio Tracks, for instance, one Group might be a sequence of all the songs, another could be a 'mellow' playlist of just acoustic numbers, and a third might be a 'party' playlist of just dance Tracks. Groups thus allow producers to create up to nine different listening experiences drawn from one underlying set of material.

## Navigation and Program Chains

As noted earlier, DVD-Audio discs are required to include three different content directories to facilitate navigation on different types of players: SAMG is used by simple Audio-only players, AMG/AOTT is used by smart Audio-only players, and AMG/AVTT is used by players that have video output (Audio-with-Video players and Universal players).

In players that use AVTT, navigation is supported via a visual menu like those used in DVD-Video (the AMGM in DVD-Audio is analogous to the VMGM in DVD-Video). AOTT machines cannot use visual menus (they have no video output), but the underlying method of enabling navigation is the same. As with DVD-Video players, navigation of the content referenced in both AVTT and AOTT is based on Program Chains (PGCs), which are instructions that tell the player what to play and when to play it.

Just as video PGCs point to VOBs, audio PGCs direct the player to AOBs. If a given AOB is to be accompanied by still images, the audio PGC will also point to the appropriate ASVU (collection of stills).

On many DVD-Audio discs, all the audio in a given Group will utilize the same channel assignment and audio attributes, and in this case that Group would normally be comprised of a single PGC. There may be Groups, however, where one or more song is available in different mixes: one for playback in stereo settings and the other in a multichannel environment. Two different PGCs would be created, one for stereo and one for multichannel. During playback the player would choose which PGC to play, depending on the playback environment.

The DVD-Audio specification includes a set of Navigation Commands for use in audio PGCs, as well as General and System parameters that are stored in player memory. As with DVD-Video, the commands are broken into various categories (Link, Jump, GoTo, SetSystem, Set and Compare), but the navigation commands supported in DVD-Audio are a subset of the DVD-Video set. Presumably that is because the Group is intended to be DVD-Audio's primary mechanism for defining a specific path through all the available content on the disc. The availability of nine Groups allows navigation that is far more varied than that of CD-Audio, but the possibilities are more limited than in DVD-Video.

Among the most important navigational constraints in DVD-Audio are those relating to movement within a Group. A user may enter a Group at any point by selecting a specific Track. But once playback has started within a given Group, that Group will continue playing in order through to the end, unless the user exits playback by using the MENU or GROUP key on the remote to go to the Album's main menu. The specification makes no provision for linking directly from a given Group to content outside that Group.

# Using video in DVD-Audio

One important aspect of DVD-Audio Groups is that they may include not only audio tracks drawn from Audio Object Sets (AOBS), but also Video Title Sets (VTS) from a disc's optional Video zone. A VTS on a DVD-Audio disc is similar to a VTS on a DVD-Video disc, but there are a number of important distinctions in the video capabilities of the two formats. For one thing, the Video Title Sets on a DVD-Audio disc do not each include an individual menu (VTSM); the only menu in the Video zone on a DVD-Audio disc is the VMGM.

Another distinction is in the audio format required for video soundtracks. As noted above, the DVD-Audio specification requires that every audio program (AOBS audio) include a PCM stream (this is the only audio type for which player support is mandated). This rule may or may not apply to the soundtracks of any video on the disc, depending on the player types for which the video's soundtrack is intended.

During the DVD-Audio production process, the producer decides whether or not the soundtrack of any VTS on the disc will play back on Audio-only players. If so (an AOTT/AVTT VTS), the VTS must follow the same audio requirements as an audio program (one mandatory PCM stream plus one optional additional stream). If the VTS soundtrack is not intended for playback on Audio-only players (an AVTT-only VTS), a PCM stream is not required (either PCM or Dolby Digital may be used).

**Table 5.8** Audio format requirements for video soundtracks in DVD-Audio vary depending on whether the type of Video Title Set used allows playback on an Audio-only player.

|  | **AOTT/AVTT VTS** | **AVTT-ONLY VTS** |
|---|---|---|
| Playable on Audio-only player? | Yes | No |
| Required audio format | Linear PCM | Dolby Digital or LPCM |
| Optional audio format | Dolby Digital | Dolby Digital or LPCM |
| LPCM parameters | max. channels @ 48 kHz: 8 max. channels @ 96 kHz: 2 bits: 16, 20 or 24 max. bit-rate: 6.1444 Mbps | same as AOTT/AVTT |
| Dolby Digital parameters | max. channels: 5.1 max. bit-rate: 448 kbps | same as AOTT/AVTT |

The DVD-Audio specification also requires that if a given type of player is able to play some of the content in a Group, it must be able to play all of the content in that Group. This means that a Group which includes a VTS that is not enabled for playback on Audio-only players may not also contain AOBS audio (which plays on Audio-only players). In effect, videos that are not enabled for (audio) playback on Audio-only players must be segregated into their own Group(s).

## Video capabilities

Another distinction between video on a DVD-Video disc and video on DVD-Audio is found in the capabilities of video PGCs (which are used to control which VOBs should be played under which conditions). The features available to control VOBs in DVD-Audio are a subset of those available on a DVD-Video disc. The degree to which the video feature set is different depends on the context in which the video is used.

We learned earlier that, conceptually, a Video zone on a DVD-Video disc is made up of distinct domains: a Video Manager (VMG) and a series of Video Title Sets, each comprising a Video Title Set Menu (VTSM) and one or more Video Titles (VTT). While the main video content of a DVD-Video disc is normally stored in the Title Sets, the VMG contains the VMG menu (VMGM), which may use either still images or motion video (VOBs) for their backgrounds. Thus, VOBs may be used in both the Menu and Title domains of the Video zone.

If a Video zone is present on a DVD-Audio disc, motion video may once again be used in either the zone's Menu or Title domains. But the Menu domain of the Video zone is never seen during playback of the disc on any type of DVD-Audio player (including Universal); it is present only to allow the disc's Video Title Sets to be viewed on a DVD-Video player. On DVD-Audio players, the viewer sees, instead, the visual menus in the AMG domain of the Audio zone.

Like VMG Menus, AMG Menus may use motion video backgrounds. The only domain on a DVD-Audio disc from which motion video is never referenced is Audio Title (ATT). In short then, on a DVD-Audio disc, video may be used in the AMG Menu (AMGM), the VMG Menu, or a Video Title (Video Title Set Menus, as noted earlier, do not exist in DVD-Audio).

The domain in which the DVD-Audio specification is most restrictive with video (compared to DVD-Video) is VTS. Parental control and seamless branching are not supported. Also, VTS PGCs in DVD-Audio do not include pre-commands or post-commands, and the use of dummy PGCs is not supported. Thus Video Title Sets on DVD-Audio discs are less capable of complex interactivity than those on DVD-Video discs. It is possible to create complex interactivity in the AMGM, where features such as pre- and post-commands are supported. However, this is not the intended purpose of the AMG domain.

Two additional notes about video on DVD-Audio discs: A DVD-Audio disc may contain DVD-Video content in its menus that is not accessible during playback on a DVD-Audio player. That is because the contents of the VMG menu – including any motion video therein – is never seen by an audio player. If desired, the AMG menu and VMG menu might each have a completely different look and feel, including the use of different motion video (if any).

It is also possible to create a DVD-Audio disc that plays the same content on either a DVD-Video player or a DVD-Audio player (Audio-with-Video or Universal). In other words, the presence of AOBS audio is not required. In this case, all the content (other than menus) would be Video Title Sets with PCM audio. This content would be accessed through AMGM on an audio player and VMGM on a video player. How much of this material would also play on an Audio-only player would depend on whether or not Audio-only playback is enabled for the Video Title Sets.

## An example DVD-Audio title

To see how all these audio and video options might work in practice, let us consider how a typical CD release with a dozen songs might be organized if it were released as a DVD-Audio title. Group 1 on the DVD might be the same material in the same sequence as the CD release, but in multichannel surround. Each song could be accompanied by a browseable slide show allowing the listener to navigate to different Index points in the song by clicking on lyrics. Group 2 could be a dance version of the album, with ballads dropped and longer 'club' mixes substituted for several of the other songs. Group 3 might be a collection of three or four music videos produced for the album, each enabled for playback on Audio-only players. And Group 4 might be a mini-documentary including interviews with the band (with playback on Audio-only players disabled).

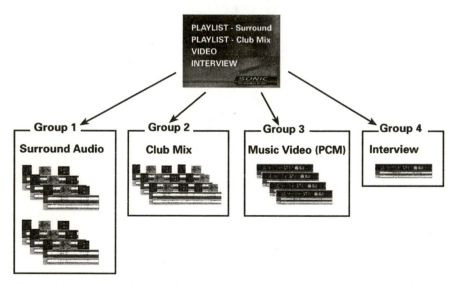

**Figure 5.11** An example DVD-Audio title with four Groups, two made up of audio content with still graphics, and two made up of video content.

Taking advantage of the disc's DVD-Others zone, meanwhile, would open up even more creative, promotional and commercial opportunities when the title is placed in a DVD-ROM drive. The disc might contain a custom browser programed to take the user to the artist's section of the label's

Web site. There the user might hear song samples from the band's other albums, order albums and other merchandise online, check a tour schedule and order tickets, or send fan e-mail to the band. Combining the flexibility of the DVD-Audio format with the underlying capabilities of DVD-ROM, the possibilities for DVD-Audio discs become nearly unlimited.

# Part II

# DVD production

# Chapter 6

# The DVD production process

DVD is a new breed of delivery medium for entertainment and information, and it brings with it new requirements that promise fundamentally to change conventional production processes.

Before DVD, the process of preparing a film or video program for home video release was often quite straightforward, sometimes simply a matter of transferring from one medium to another. The professional skills involved were focused primarily on yielding copies that were as close in quality as possible to the original source, even though the delivery medium was different (not an easy task for VHS releases).

With the advent of DVD-Video, the preparation of commercial video titles has become far more complex, involving new skills such as video encoding and navigational design. The introduction of DVD-Audio will no doubt bring about similar changes in the 'pre-mastering' of audio releases (the production step just before the project is sent to the replication plant).

The recording industry has traditionally thought of pre-mastering as a set of fine adjustments to the audio program, a final 'polish' which takes place after the main creative elements are in place. The music being pre-mastered, it was assumed, would eventually be experienced by the listener as a stereo (or occasionally mono) presentation.

DVD-Audio introduces many new variables into music title preparation. Now, a given project may be presented not only in stereo, but also in one of many variations of multichannel surround sound; music may now be presented as an audio-only program, or with text, graphics or motion video.

These new possibilities will encourage producers to think of multiple media and multiple presentation settings, and to try to create experiences which take advantage of all available creative opportunities.

Although it is perhaps early to make sweeping predictions about exactly how DVD-Audio will alter music production and pre-mastering, the related area of DVD-Video production is already three years old. Guided by the DVD-Video experience, it is possible – while mindful of the distinct considerations involved in music and video projects – to lay out an overall approach to production for both formats.

# Production steps

DVD-Audio provides the richest and potentially most complicated set of possible media types, while DVD-Video offers the greatest potential for complex interactivity. However, much of the production process involved is common to both formats. To cover the whole range of possibilities, we will assume (unless otherwise noted) that any examples given below pertain to combination DVD-Video and DVD-Audio titles.

The DVD production process may be broken down into a series of steps: project planning and 'Bit Budget™'; asset preparation; authoring (media integration); proofing (preview); formatting; output and testing. Much of the process is iterative, with cycles of asset preparation, authoring and proofing followed by re-editing and/or re-authoring until all aspects of the project are approved.

While the different processes involved in DVD production are not necessarily required to take place in the same physical location, the more tightly they can be integrated and controlled, the more efficient the title production process becomes. In an integrated, multistation production environment, processes which are described below as being consecutive (for the sake of clarity) may in fact be handled in parallel, speeding project throughput.

# Project planning

The first step in DVD production is to define the scope and basic structure of the project. This may range from a simple Audio-only title, with traditional stereo presentation, to an elaborate music and video title with multiple

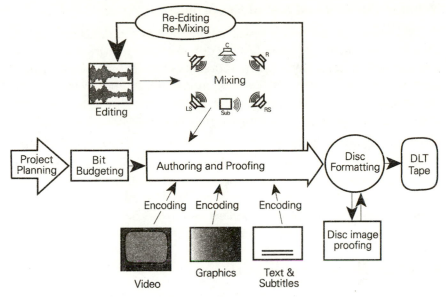

**Figure 6.1** An integrated, multistation DVD production environment.

still-graphics shows and assorted video content. For successful project management, it is essential to first define the content and organization of the project, and to develop a Project Template.

## Questions to ask

As in any planning process, one of the most effective ways to define the scope of a DVD project is to be sure that you have thought through the answers to a series of basic questions:

### What platforms do you want the project to play back on?

A DVD disc may be designed to play in any one of several playback settings (DVD-Video player, DVD-Video and DVD-Audio Universal player, DVD-Audio Audio-only players, or PC-based DVD-ROM), or it may be intended to work in all of these. The behaviour of the title will vary depending on the setting, and so it is very important to consider what each DVD platform would bring to your material, what the limitations of each platform are, and how designing for several settings would impact the title's playback in each.

## What is the look and feel of the project?

A DVD title's look and feel is largely determined by the direction taken in menu design. As the number of DVD-Video titles on the market grows, and the production community learns more about DVD's possibilities, both creative and competitive marketing considerations are driving a trend towards a richer, more complex title experience. However, the more elaborate the title design, the longer it may take in production.

For example, menus with motion-video backgrounds and surround sound may be more exciting than menus with background stills, yet they require more disc space and greater authoring skills. On the other hand, while using a just a few still menus might be less flashy from an interactive standpoint, it may be the most convenient and effective way to connect the user to the disc's content, and it can make title production much faster.

## How interactive is the project?

If a project is a simple linear-play, Audio-only DVD-Audio title, interactivity is not a major concern in the project planning stage. On the other hand, a DVD-Video game title with intense interactivity will be far too complex to simply improvise on the fly. The more interactive a title, or the more media elements it incorporates, the more crucial it is to create a highly detailed project template in advance, to guide the production process. This will also allow accurate appraisal of the time and resources that will be required to complete the title.

## How many types of audio will be presented?

The range of audio choices in DVD is very diverse. It is important to determine as early as possible whether audio will be presented in stereo, surround sound, or both, and what resolutions (sample-rate, word-length) will be used. These decisions are critical for bit budgeting, as well as for the creation and management of the project's assets.

## Will video be used?

The use of video will have a major impact on the allocation of bandwidth on the disc, as well as on the available audio types and combinations.

## What about text and multiple languages?

Given the various text-handling capabilities of DVD formats (including subtitles and Real Time Text), title producers are likely to find many different ways to utilize text. Each additional language used may involve translation, editing and synchronization with audio and video programs.

## Will the title be a hybrid DVD, possibly including Web connectivity?

Hybrid DVD titles combine the DVD-Video and/or DVD-Audio programme stored on disc with additional material stored in the DVD-Others zone, where it may be accessed from a DVD-ROM drive. This approach can affect project planning on several levels. First, the amount of storage space on the disc that is available for DVD-Video or DVD-Audio will be reduced by the presence of other material. The practical effect of this depends on the kind and amount of added material; text will take very little space, while large amounts of graphics, audio or video will eat up a noticeable amount of the overall storage capacity.

Hybrid titles may also require close coordination between the DVD production team and the interactive multimedia design team that creates the added content. A Web-connected title, for instance, may involve the development of a consistent look and feel that works both for DVD menus and for Web pages that are accessed via a browser on the disc. If the title is an eDVD™, with support for DVD-Video content that plays from a Web page in a browser, the production team will need to work together closely to ensure smooth integration of both visual and interactive design.

## *Template and assets*

As the answers to the questions above become known, it is possible to develop an overview of what the title will consist of and how it will be organized. Variously referred to as a template, flowchart or storyboard for the title, this document serves as the blueprint to be referred to throughout the production process.

From the Project Template, a list of required source assets may be derived. Assets will include audio sources, video sources, graphic files, text and subtitle files.

As an example, let us consider a hybrid DVD-Video/DVD-Audio title designed for both the US and Japanese markets. The title is made up of two main parts. A 75-minute audio segment will consist of 15 tracks in high-resolution (24-bit/96 kHz) PCM surround sound, accompanied by still images, subpictures, and text. In addition, a 90-minute concert video documentary will use a Dolby Digital 5.1 surround soundtrack. Menus will use still backgrounds rather than motion video.

For this production one would need the source assets as shown in Table 6.1.

**Table 6.1** Source assets for example DVD title.

| | |
|---|---|
| Audio | Source for 6-track music program (24-bit/96 kHz) |
| | Source for 5.1 channel video soundtrack |
| Video | Digital video source tapes |
| Stills | TIFF graphic files for still images |
| Menus | TIFF graphic files for menu backgrounds |
| Text | English text lyrics with time references |
| | Japanese text lyrics with time references |

# The Bit Budget™

Once the project definition is complete, the next step is to allocate the disc's data bandwidth (bit-rate) and overall data capacity to the various audio, video, graphic and subpicture elements included in the asset list. This process involves quite a bit of calculation, which an advanced DVD authoring package should handle automatically (Sonic DVD Creator, for instance, dynamically recalculates the Bit Budget™ as the title is designed). However, working through the process here will give us a good feel for how it affects the content and quality of a finished title. Depending on the results, a producer may even decide to beef up or scale back the amount of extra material included on a disc, or to change the disc capacity used.

Although DVD storage capacity is significantly greater than CD, it is still limited to 4.7, 8.5, 9.4, or 17 GB of data, depending on the number of sides and layers of the disc. These capacities govern how much audio and video may be stored on a given title. At the same time, a standard DVD player has a maximum combined data delivery rate of under 10 Megabits per second (Mbps) for all video, audio, and subpictures assets (such as subtitles).

Keeping in mind these two basic limitations – disc capacity and maximum data-rate – one can start with the length of the program, the audio configuration(s), and the size of the disc, and from there calculate how the bits will be allocated to video, audio, subpictures, and interactivity. Remember that data-rate and data capacity measurements in DVD are based on simple multiples (1 KB equals 1000 bytes) rather than computing conventions (1 KB equals 1024 bytes). Thus a 4.7 GB DVD-5 disc holds 4.7 billion bytes (which would be expressed as 4.38 GB in conventional computer terminology).

## Bit Budget calculation

Bit budgeting generally begins with audio tracks first, based on the audio configurations defined in the asset list. This is because, in many cases (particularly with uncompressed PCM) the bit-rate requirement of a given audio stream flows directly from its audio attributes (sample-rate, word-length, channel configuration). With video, on the other hand, the MPEG-2 format allows us to specify a target bit-rate and then encode the video to that target.

Keep in mind that the higher the video bit-rate, the better the resulting video image will generally be. The point of figuring the audio first is to assess how high we will be able to set the bit-rate used during video encoding, because we want to be sure that the audio formats we use during the video portions of our content leave enough bandwidth for the video to be encoded at presentable quality. Bit budgeting will also help us determine whether to use CBR (Constant Bit-rate) or VBR (Variable Bit-rate) video encoding. If we use VBR, we will need to calculate both the average and the maximum bit-rate setting.

Because of the complexity and size of our example project, we will base our Bit Budget on a DVD-9 (8.5 GB capacity).

### Step 1 – Capacity

We start with a look at the total delivery capability of DVD-9.

**8 500 000 000 (bits) × 8 (bit/bytes)/1 000 000 (bits/megabit)**

**= 68 000 Megabits available**

To be safe, we should allow some room for overhead. Experience has shown that it is prudent to reserve about 4 per cent of the disc capacity for menu graphics, navigation information, and extra cushion.

**68 000 Megabits × 0.96 (100% less 4%) = 65 280 Megabits**

## Step 2 – High-resolution audio program

We next determine the data requirements for the high-resolution audio program. Without packing, we would calculate six channels of 24-bit/96 kHz audio as follows:

**96 kHz × 24 bits per sample × 60 seconds per minute × 75 minutes × 6 tracks**

**= 62 208 Megabits**

As we learned earlier, however, six channels of 24-bit/96 kHz audio requires a bandwidth of 13.8 Mbps, while the maximum data-rate of a DVD-Audio player is 9.6 Mbps. Thus we need to encode the audio using MLP (lossless packing). This makes bit budgeting a bit tricky, because the exact amount of data-rate savings achieved by MLP is not completely predictable; the efficiency of the algorithm varies based on the complexity of the audio program itself.

We do have a general idea, however, of the minimum compression that MLP offers, so for planning purposes we will assume 40 per cent savings (final bandwidth equal to 60 per cent of the input bandwidth). It is likely that the actual packing will yield even lower data-rates, but it is wise to be conservative. Otherwise we may discover late in the project that we have over-estimated the efficiency of packing, which would mean that the project would not fit in the available space.

**62 208 Megabits × 0.6 (compression ratio)**

**= 37 325 Megabits (high-resolution MLP audio)**

The use of MLP not only brings the data-rate down below 9.6 Mbps, but also means that we now have some room left over on the disc for the video portion of the program.

In our asset list we also specified still images and subtitles (two tracks) to accompany the high-resolution audio program. Let us assume one still image per track, at a rate of 1 Megabit (125 KB) per still.

**Still images: 1 Megabit × 15 tracks = 15 Megabits**

Subtitles require a bandwidth of 0.04 Mbps per track, or 0.08 Mbps overall for our two subtitle tracks.

**Subtitles: 0.08 Mbps × 60 seconds per minute × 75 minutes**

**= 360 Megabits**

Thus the total capacity allocated to the high-resolution audio section of the title is:

37 325 Mb (Audio) + 15 Mb (Stills) + 360 Mb (Subtitles) = 37 700 Mb

## Step 3 – Video program, non-video elements

At this point we can calculate the capacity remaining for the 90-minute long video portion of our program. First we take the total disc capacity (less overhead) and subtract the bits allocated to the high-resolution audio program:

65 280 – 37 700 = 27 580 Megabits

We have chosen to have a Dolby Digital 5.1 channel soundtrack with our video. Audio streams in Dolby Digital (AC-3) format use a constant rate of 0.192 Mbps for stereo and from 0.384 up to 0.448 Mbps for surround. The most common rate for surround is 0.384 Mbps, so our Dolby Digital stream requires:

0.384 Mbps × 60 seconds per minute × 90 minutes = 2074 Megabits

As in the music program, subtitles require a bandwidth of 0.04 Mbps per track, or 0.08 Mbps overall for our two subtitle tracks.

Subtitles: 0.08 Mbps × 60 seconds per minute × 90 minutes

= 432 Megabits

Thus the non-video data requirements for the video program are:

2074 Mb (Dolby Digital) + 432 Mb (Subtitles) = 2506 Mb

## Step 4 – Video program, video element

To find the capacity left for our video element, we subtract the non-video elements from the overall capacity allocated to the video program:

27 580 Megabits – 2506 Megabits = 25 074 Megabits

For the best video image quality, we want to encode the video at the highest-possible average bit-rate. To determine how high the average bit-rate can be, we divide the available capacity by the length of the program (in seconds).

90 minutes × 60 seconds = 5400 seconds

25 074 Megabits / 5400 seconds = 4.64 Mbps

## Step 5 – Peak and target bit-rates

Finally, we need to see how this average video bit-rate of 4.64 Mbps compares with the maximum available video bit-rate, which is the bandwidth of DVD-Audio players (9.6 Mbps) minus the data-rate of the non-video elements of the video program.

9.6 Mbps – 0.384 Mbps (Dolby Digital 5.1 stream)

– 0.08 Mbps (two subtitle streams) = 9.136 Mbps

Now that we know both the average video bit-rate and the maximum available video bit-rate for this program, we can evaluate whether to use Constant Bit-rate (CBR) or Variable Bit-rate (VBR) encoding. With VBR, static, easy-to-encode scenes will be encoded at relatively low bit-rates, and the bits saved will be allocated (up to the maximum rate) to improve the quality of fast-moving, visually complex scenes that require more bits for good quality. In this case, with the maximum higher than the average, we should be able optimize to the image quality of our video by using VBR encoding with a target bit-rate of 4.64 Mbps and a peak bit-rate of 9.136 Mbps.

If our example disc had used much shorter video material, or much higher data-rates for the non-video elements of the video program (stereo PCM streams in three different languages, for instance), the maximum available video bit-rate could have been lower than the average bit-rate. In that case, the actual encoding rate used would be limited by bandwidth to the lower figure, and there would be no advantage to using VBR rather than CBR.

**Table 6.2** The bit-rate available for encoding video depends on both the program length and the bit-rates of the audio and subtitle tracks. Based on a 4 per cent margin for overhead and an audio/subtitle bit-rate of 0.928 Mbps (one Dolby Digital surround track, two Dolby Digital stereo tracks, and four subtitle tracks), this table shows how the bit-rate available for video on a DVD-5 declines as program length increases.

| Length of Program (minutes) | Maximum Available Bit-rate on a DVD-5 (Mbps) | Audio/Subpicture Bit-rate (Mbps) | Average Video Bit-rate (Mbps) |
|---|---|---|---|
| 60 | 9.8 | 0.928 | 8.872 |
| 90 | 6.684 | 0.928 | 5.756 |
| 120 | 5.013 | 0.928 | 4.085 |
| 150 | 4.011 | 0.928 | 3.083 |

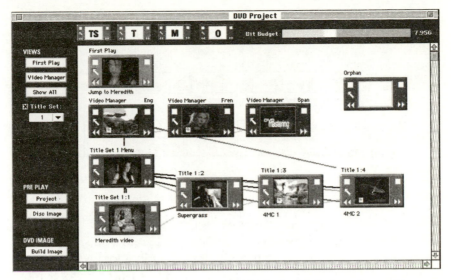

**Figure 6.2** Sonic DVD Creator with integrated Bit Budget™ display at upper right.

As noted earlier, these types of calculations – tedious and time-consuming to perform manually – are amongst the functions handled behind-the-scenes in a well-designed DVD authoring tool. In Sonic DVD Creator, for instance, a built-in display tracks the Bit Budget as assets are linked to the title, helping to ensure that the project stays within defined limits. The DVD Creator screen showing the Bit Budget meter is shown in Figure 6.2.

## Multi-angle considerations

One additional consideration in arriving at a Bit Budget which applies to DVD-Video discs is the extent to which the format's multi-angle feature is used in the title. Multi-angle video allows the viewer to switch seamlessly between up to nine different angles.

One would expect that as more angles are used in a given stream, the data-rate available for each angle would be divided into smaller and smaller increments. Instead, however, multi-angle video is enabled by 'interleaving' VOBs. Depending on the angle currently selected by the viewer, the player skips over blocks of information that contain the data for the angles that are not being displayed. This allows the bit-rate for each of the angles to remain relatively high.

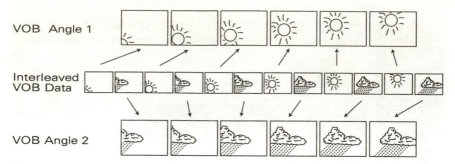

VOB Angle 1

Interleaved
VOB Data

VOB Angle 2

**Figure 6.3** The interleaving of angles in multi-angle video.

When calculating video encoding rates for material that will be used in a multi-angle setting, the maximum combined data-rate (video, audio and subpictures) drops from the normal 9.8 Mbps (9.6 Mbps for DVD-Audio) to as low as 7 Mbps (although it may be possible to use up to 8 Mbps depending on the location of the VOB on the disc and the maximum jump distance). In other words, for a given set of audio and subtitle tracks, the maximum video data-rate for each angle will be between 1.8 and 2.8 Mbps lower when encoding for multi-angle playback. It is also important to recognize that each angle has its own separate audio and subtitle streams (quite possibly identical to the audio and subtitles for the other angles), and that storing those additional streams on disc reduces the available disc space.

# Chapter 7

# Asset preparation

Asset preparation involves creating or obtaining all the individual media elements of a title that are specified on the asset list, and converting those elements into the form needed to integrate them into a DVD title.

Asset preparation is always a major concern in the DVD production process, but the size of the job varies depending on the number of elements involved and in what form they are available. In some cases a DVD's content will largely be re-purposed from elements already created for use in other contexts, while in other situations all the elements may be created entirely from scratch.

In a typical scenario, different aspects of production are often handled in different facilities: the video is edited at a post production house, the sound is mixed in a recording studio, and the background graphics for menus are designed by a graphic designer. It is crucial that the production professionals at each of these various facilities understand the specific requirements that the materials they prepare will have to meet in order to be useable for DVD. Otherwise it is quite possible that significant time and money will be needed to redo elements that are not compatible with, or optimized for inclusion in, a DVD project.

## Video assets

Video is the core media type of DVD-Video, and it also plays an important role in DVD-Audio, where it is used to display still pictures, menus and optional motion video. Much of the preparation of video assets for DVD involves tasks commonly associated with video production and post production. These may include editing for home video release, transfer from film to video (telecine), standards conversion (NTSC to PAL or vice versa), or even shooting interviews and other documentary material for small features included as value-added content.

A discussion of post production techniques is beyond the scope of this book, but it is important to realize that every operation performed on the video material carries with it the risk of degradation of signal quality or the introduction of noise. Undesirable in any context, signal degradation and noise can be especially problematic in terms of maintaining the image quality of material that will undergo video compression. Thus it is crucial to use the best available equipment and techniques at every step in the production of a master that will be used for DVD.

Ideally, video destined for DVD should be of master quality and delivered in a component broadcast format such as D1 or Digital Betacam, which will yield much better results than a composite video format. Alternatively, if the video has been prepared on a non-linear editing (NLE) system, best results may be obtained by direct digital transcoding into MPEG-2 from video files, without first laying the material to tape. (All of Sonic's DVD authoring applications support this mode of importing and encoding video and audio which have been prepared on popular NLE packages from Avid, Media 100, and other QuickTime-based video editing systems.)

## MPEG compression

High-quality MPEG video compression – developed by the Motion Picture Experts Group – is the enabling technology for video on DVD. While MPEG

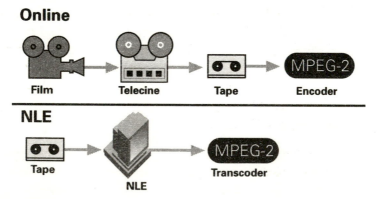

**Figure 7.1** Video encoded to MPEG-2 may result from either of two different video production chains.

compression is a very complicated topic, a basic overview here should be helpful in understanding video preparation for DVD.

Video compression is used in DVD because uncompressed digital video demands huge amounts of data bandwidth and storage. Uncompressed 'studio-quality' video (ITU-R BT.601–5, 4:4:2 sampling at 10 bits) generates data at a rate of over 200 Mbps, meaning that a two-hour program would consume over 200 GB of storage space (without accounting for audio), vastly exceeding the storage available on any DVD disc (4.7–17 GB).

MPEG compression is based largely on the observation that in motion pictures there is typically a high degree of redundancy – both spatial (within a given image) and temporal (between successive images). In part, MPEG reduces the amount of data by minimizing the extent to which this redundant information is stored during encoding. Assuming that the decoding system is able to accurately recreate that information during playback, data bandwidth and storage requirements can be significantly reduced with little or no impact on perceived image quality.

In brief, the encoding process begins with intra-frame compression, which operates on each video frame individually. The picture is broken into a grid of small blocks, and the colour information present in each block is re-coded to express redundant information more efficiently.

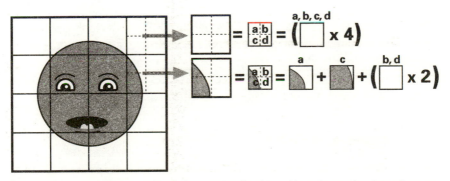

**Figure 7.2** In intra-frame compression, areas of a given video picture that have the same colour value are re-coded to express redundant values more efficiently.

Depending on the target bit-rate, intra-frame compression may also involve coding adjacent colours that are similar to one another as if they are the same colour. This increases redundancy and thereby decreases data-rate requirements, but it also results in some loss of detail. The extent to which this loss is noticeable depends on both the amount of compression used and the specific program being compressed.

Intra-frame compression is followed by inter-frame compression, in which a series of adjacent frames are compared and only the information necessary to describe the differences between successive frames is retained. When the encoded material is played back, a decoder extrapolates from the stored information to re-create a complete set of discrete frames.

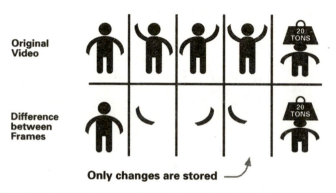

Original Video

Difference between Frames

**Only changes are stored**

**Figure 7.3** Rather than storing every frame in its entirety, inter-frame compression stores a series of frames as information about frame-to-frame changes.

Note that the effectiveness of MPEG video compression is highly dependent on the video material being compressed. For example, a fast-paced, visually complex action sequence has comparatively little frame-to-frame redundant information. That makes it more difficult to compress than other material, meaning that it will require a higher bit-rate to re-create it accurately.

## Frame types and GOPs

An MPEG-2 video stream is normally made up of three types of pictures, defined as I-pictures, B-pictures, and P-pictures. I-pictures (intra) are compressed using intra-frame techniques only, meaning that the information stored is complete enough to decode the picture without reference to any adjacent frames. B (bi-directional) and P (predictive) pictures, on the other hand, are encoded using inter-frame compression to store 'difference information' (frame-to-frame changes). B- and P-pictures require much less data capacity to store, but they can only be reconstructed by referring to the I-pictures around them.

**Table 7.1** The three types of MPEG-2 pictures.

| Picture type | Definition |
|---|---|
| I | I-pictures are encoded using intra-frame compression, and contain all the information needed to reconstruct an individual frame of video. |
| P | P-pictures (predictive) are more compressed than I-pictures. They are reconstructed based on the nearest previous I- or P-picture, and provide a reference for the calculation of B-pictures. |
| B | B-pictures (bi-directional) use the least amount of data. They are reconstructed by referring to information in both a previous and a subsequent frame. |

In an MPEG stream, the I-, B-, and P-pictures created during encoding occur in a specific sequence referred to as a 'Group of Pictures' (GOP), the smallest addressable unit of MPEG video. The I-pictures serve as reference points that allow the decoder to interpret the difference information representing the B- and P-pictures. MPEG supports the use of a variety of different GOP structures in the same stream, and each GOP includes a 'header' with information about the structure that follows. A typical DVD-Video stream might be made up primarily of GOPs with a size of 15, using a picture sequence of I-B-B-P-B-B-P-B-B-P-B-B-P-B-B-I.

GOP structures are of more than academic interest in DVD production. For example, a common technique used to improve subjective compressed image quality is to impose or 'force' I-pictures at points where there are large differences between successive frames (e.g. scene changes). Also, chapter points and cell boundaries must align on GOP boundaries for video decoding to work smoothly when jumping to an entry point. This may require re-encoding some portion of the material at these locations using a different GOP structure. (Advanced DVD packages that support segment-based re-encoding will avert the need to re-encode an entire program.)

## VBR encoding

DVD supports the use of both Constant Bit-rate (CBR) and Variable Bit-rate (VBR) MPEG video encoding. VBR is used extensively, particularly for programs such as feature films which are more than one hour long. As we learned earlier, video source material can vary dramatically in its complexity, and hence in the difficulty of achieving substantial savings in bit-rate without degrading image quality. VBR addresses this problem by allocating fewer bits to those sequences which are comparatively easy to compress, and more bits to those which are harder to compress.

If artfully done, VBR can greatly improve the image quality that may be achieved at a given bit-rate, or, alternatively, substantially increase the amount of video that may be stored on a given disc. As always, the exact benefits vary depending on the specific program material, but in general the application of VBR techniques may result in a reduction of 50 per cent in the space utilized.

Consider, for example, a two-hour movie to be released on DVD-5. All told, audio, subtitles and overhead might take 0.8 Mbps of bandwidth and 0.9 GB of disc space. For video, that leaves approximately 3.8 GB of space (4.7 − 0.9) and a maximum bit-rate of 9 Mbps (9.8 − 0.8). With VBR, the video encoding parameters could be set to produce an average bit-rate of 4.22 Mbps, and a peak bit-rate of 9 Mbps. Using CBR, the entire movie would have to be encoded at 4.22 Mbps, without the benefit of the 9 Mbps peak rate for difficult scenes.

## Inverse telecine and pre-processing

We know that MPEG video encoding achieves its high compression ratios by eliminating redundant information, and that the more redundancy can be eliminated, the more bits will be available to accurately capture the remaining picture information. That is the motivation for using both inverse telecine and video pre-processing.

Inverse telecine removes redundancy introduced into NTSC video during the film-to-video (telecine) transfer process. Because film runs at 24 frames per second and NTSC video runs at 30 frames (or 60 interlaced fields) per second, the conventional telecine process assigns successive film frames first to two and then to three video fields. This means that every fifth video field resulting from the transfer contains completely redundant information. Detecting and extracting this redundant field yields an overall gain of 20 per cent in compression (or better image quality at the same data-rate).

A nice side-benefit of inverse telecine is that when stepping frame-by-frame through a sequence the viewer will see precisely 24 full frames for each second of video material (if the process has been performed accurately).

In real-world production, material that originates on film is often edited after transfer to video, so one can rarely assume that video retains the constant

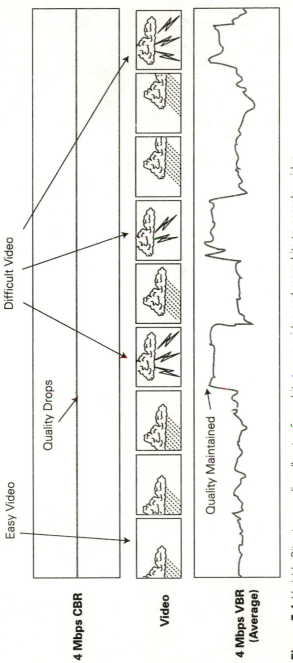

**4 Mbps CBR**

Easy Video

Quality Drops

Difficult Video

**Video**

**4 Mbps VBR (Average)**

Quality Maintained →

**Figure 7.4** Variable Bit-rate encoding allocates fewer bits to easy video and more bits to complex video.

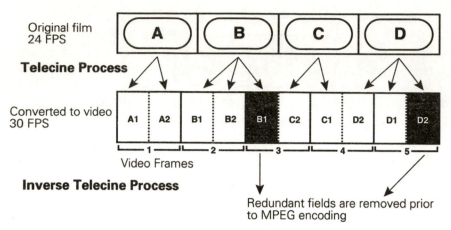

**Figure 7.5** Inverse telecine removes redundant frames introduced in telecine (NTSC).

3-2-3-2 cadence of the original telecine transfer. This is what makes inverse telecine a demanding process for an MPEG compression system. It is important that an advanced encoding package is used, one that automatically examines every successive video field to spot changes in the cadence.

In video pre-processing, a digital noise reducer or low-pass filter is used to reduce high-energy noise in the video signal prior to encoding. Noise may be introduced into the video signal by equipment used upstream from the compression process which is not aligned or functioning properly. Alternatively, it may result from the nature of the source image itself: grainy film, dust, snowfall, or textured surfaces such as a white stucco wall. Such noise tends to be random rather than consistent from frame to frame.

When random noise is reduced by pre-processing, the video signal has greater frame-to-frame consistency. The more redundancy, the easier it is for the MPEG encoder to maintain image quality at a given bit-rate.

## The encoding process

Encoding high-quality video for DVD requires powerful MPEG-2 compression technology. These encoders must be able to handle VBR encoding, inverse telecine and video at multiple aspect ratios. At the same time, effective tools will be designed to make the compression process easy and intuitive for the operator.

The quality of the source material directly affects the quality of the final MPEG-2 stream. Good results will be achieved from video that either originates (is shot) in a CCIR-601 digital video format such as D1, Digital Betacam, or DCT tape, or is transferred from film directly to these formats. A higher-resolution source such as an HDTV master is even better. The highest possible resolution should be maintained at each step that the video goes through before MPEG encoding.

In theory, VBR encoding may be carried out in a single pass. In practice, however, that approach would offer little opportunity for the encoding system to gather the information it needs to analyse the program material and optimize the allocation of bits. While VBR may be performed in three passes, an advanced video encoding package will be capable of achieving optimum quality in only two passes. In Sonic DVD Creator, for example, the VBR encoding process works as follows:

Pass 1   A preliminary analysis is performed of the video program, resulting in initial I-picture placement, and a profile of the program. If the user has engaged SmartCheck™, an analysis is performed that adjusts the compression algorithm to match closely the complexity of the video program. Also at this stage, 'thumbnail' pictures are generated for DVD Creator's highly graphical user interface.

Pass 2   The actual encoding is performed and an MPEG stream is deposited on the system's hard disk.

Each pass in the VBR process is done in real-time, allowing the operator to view the results of the compression process as it takes place. In a real-time networked production environment with guaranteed bandwidth, the MPEG-2 video stream can be recorded directly to a shared hard disk so that an encoded stream may be accessed across the network by other DVD production systems while it is still being encoded.

## Segment-based re-encoding

Although an MPEG-2 VBR encoder can be designed to use the best overall encoding parameters for a given video source, small segments of MPEG-2 video will usually benefit from being modified manually for maximum quality. Additionally, decisions made during the DVD production process may involve changes to the project's Bit Budget after the movie has been encoded, necessitating bit-rate changes to the MPEG-2 video stream.

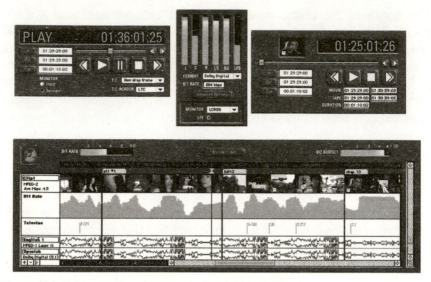

**Figure 7.6** A segment-based re-encode in Sonic DVD Creator.

The re-encoding process is analogous to the pre-mastering stage in the record industry, where changes in dynamics and equalization are applied to polish the finished program. In both cases, this fine tuning is critical to achieve professional quality output.

In DVD production, it is very important that the MPEG-2 encoding system supports the ability to select specific segments of video and re-encode them. The lack of this capability will often force users of unsophisticated MPEG-2 encoders to re-analyse and re-encode an entire movie just to implement a small change in a GOP structure or a bit-rate level. In a professional production setting, where throughput is critical, considerations of deadlines and productivity make segment-based re-encoding a virtual necessity.

# Audio preparation

The range and flexibility of audio support in both DVD-Video and DVD-Audio makes audio perhaps the most intricate area of asset preparation to cover in detail. This complexity stems not only from the encoding processes used, but also from the number and variety of simultaneous streams that may be used in a single title. We will start by looking at audio as it is used in DVD-Video and in the video content on DVD-Audio. Then we will discuss some of the additional audio considerations introduced by DVD-Audio's high-resolution and multichannel capabilities.

## Audio formats

As described earlier, PCM and Dolby Digital are the primary audio formats used in DVD, while support for additional formats is an option included in some players. In DVD-Audio, up to two simultaneous user-selected audio streams may be supplied in any given program, one of which must be PCM (linear or MLP). In DVD-Video, a video program may be accompanied by up to eight simultaneous audio streams.

In DVD-Video, Dolby Digital is supported in both NTSC and PAL countries. The use of this compressed format is not required as long as a stereo PCM track is included instead, and extensive support (described earlier) is included in the DVD-Video specification for both stereo and multichannel PCM (although player manufacturers are just now starting to show interest in the multichannel possibilities). However, because compression allows acceptable audio quality at a bit-rate far below that of PCM – thus leaving more bits available for the video – compressed audio is very widely used with video content. This means that an effective DVD-Video production package must be able to capture audio in both PCM and Dolby Digital formats.

Both Dolby Digital and MPEG audio, sometimes included as an option in PAL markets, use perceptual coding techniques to reduce the amount of data needed to represent the audio signal. These formats employ compression algorithms that discard sound from frequency bands which contain limited signal energy. They also use noise-shaping techniques to remove audio information in frequency areas where humans are least likely to notice missing sound.

As we saw during bit budgeting, each audio stream used is allocated a portion of the overall data-rate depending on its format and, in some cases, the compression settings used during audio capture. Audio streams in Dolby Digital format, for instance, use 192 Kbps for stereo and 384 to 448 Kbps for surround. Once set, the data-rate for each Dolby Digital stream is constant, meaning that the number of bits allocated to a given stream remains the same throughout the program, without regard to the complexity of the program material.

MPEG-2 audio (an extension of MPEG-1 layer II audio) may also be encoded at a constant rate, but optionally allows use of a variable bit-rate (for the same reasons that VBR is used on video). In practice, VBR audio has yet to find wide acceptance, in part because of the risk that audio and video peaks will occur simultaneously, thus pushing the overall bit-rate beyond allowable limits.

## Compressed surround sound

Either Dolby Digital or MPEG may be used to deliver audio in both stereo or surround. Dolby Digital may be used for mono, stereo or multichannel audio for up to 5.1 channels, and MPEG for up to 7.1 channels. The term '5.1 channels' means five full-range channels (left front, centre, right front, left rear, right rear) and a limited bandwidth low-frequency-effects (LFE) channel (the '.1' channel) that is frequently thought of as a sub-woofer channel.

Most DVD-Video titles today that include a surround soundtrack do so in a Dolby format, because of the large population of Dolby surround decoders in the hands of consumers. However, it is important to be aware of the distinction between Dolby Digital and Dolby Surround.

Dolby Surround is the home theatre version of the Dolby Stereo audio configuration introduced in 1976 for theatrical films. In Dolby Stereo, four

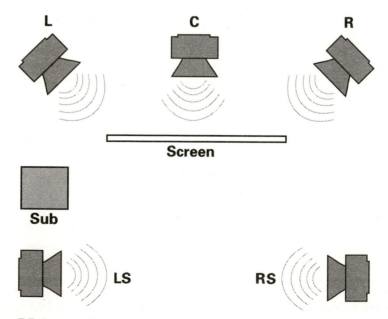

**Figure 7.7** A surround sound listening environment.

audio channels (left, centre, right and surround) are matrixed (encoded) in the analog domain into a two-channel 'Left-total, Right-total' (Lt/Rt) signal. When delivered on a consumer format such as a VHS tape, this audio signal is referred to as being in Dolby Surround. With a Dolby Pro Logic decoder (stand-alone or in a receiver) the Lt/Rt signal is decoded to its original four channels; without a decoder the two-channel signal is used for stereo playback. While Dolby Surround has been popular in the home theatre context, achieving accurate playback at home with no matrixing artifacts can be tricky.

In some cases confusion may arise because a two-channel Dolby Digital stream may be used to deliver a Dolby Surround signal that will play back through a Pro Logic decoder (a two-channel PCM stream may be used in the same way). This is not the same as a 5.1 channel Dolby Digital surround soundtrack.

An alternative compressed digital audio format for surround sound is DTS from Digital Theatre Systems. Although DTS is supported in DVD as an 'optional' audio format, the company has been successful in obtaining support from a number of consumer electronics manufacturers who include DTS decoders in their DVD players or A/V processors. It is important that a full-featured DVD authoring package be able to handle DTS files.

In concert with the perceptual coding techniques discussed earlier, compressed surround formats use a cross-correlation scheme to avoid storing information that is redundant amongst the channels. The systems also use 'fold down' mechanisms to permit a surround stream to be presented in a stereo environment (much like the SMART Content feature of DVD-Audio).

In DVD-Audio, the question of whether or not audio in a compressed surround format may be included on a given disc depends on the type of disc. Pure Audio titles currently may contain audio only in PCM format (linear or MLP); optional audio formats (if any) for these titles have not yet been defined. However, in other DVD-Audio title types (those which utilize AVTT/AOTT or AVTT-only navigation), Dolby Digital, MPEG and DTS are 'optional' formats that may be present in addition to the mandatory PCM program.

The advantage of Dolby Digital, MPEG and DTS from a DVD-Audio perspective is the relatively limited bandwidth required to support surround playback. For example, Dolby Digital 5.1 requires only about a quarter of the bandwidth needed to store 16-bit stereo PCM at 44.1 or 48 kHz. Given

**Table 7.2** Comparative bit-rates for various 5.1-channel audio formats. Six channels of 20 bit/88.2 kHz or 24 bit/96 kHz PCM would require MLP to fit within the maximum DVD-Audio bit-rate.

| Audio format | Bit-rate for 5.1 channels |
|---|---|
| Dolby Digital | 0.384–0.448 Mbps |
| DTS | 1.536 Mbps |
| PCM: 16 bit/44.1 kHz (CD resolution) Six channels, no MLP | 4.234 Mbps |
| PCM: 16 bit/48 kHz Six channels, no MLP | 4.608 Mbps |
| PCM: 20 bit/88.2 kHz Six channels, no MLP | 10.584 Mbps (exceeds maximum bit-rate) |
| PCM: 24 bit/96 kHz Six channels, no MLP | 13.824 Mbps (exceeds maximum bit-rate) |

the population of surround decoders already in the hands of consumers, it is not unlikely that some DVD-Audio producers will choose to include surround material in one or another of these compressed formats.

## Restoration, mixing and conforming

While support for surround sound enables DVD-Video as a home theatre format, it does not guarantee the ready availability of surround soundtracks. Dolby Stereo was introduced into theatres over two decades ago, but only in recent years have films been released theatrically in digital surround formats such as Dolby Digital, DTS and SDDS (Sony Dynamic Digital Sound).

Creating a 5.1 mix is particularly problematic for older films, where the original sound elements may be lost, or have deteriorated over time. In many cases the only soundtrack available is the mono optical track from a release print. Where a soundtrack or individual elements are in less than pristine condition, Sonic's NoNoise® audio restoration technology may be used to minimize crackle, clicks, pops, hiss and other undesirable artifacts. If audio is available from more than one source, the best parts of each available soundtrack may have to be restored and then edited together to create a complete program.

Where only a mono or stereo soundtrack is available, it is up to the content owner or title producer to decide whether it makes sense to create a 5.1

mix through selective panning across a multichannel sound field. Even where the stems used to create the final mix of a film are available and in good shape, the producer must decide whether the cost of remixing the material is warranted by the aesthetic or marketing benefits of doing so. Thus, the choice between stereo, Dolby Surround or a 5.1 channel surround format will continue to be made on a case-by-case basis.

If a 5.1 channel mix has already been prepared for theatrical release (which may well be the case for recent films), that mix would normally be included on DVD. However, it may need further audio mastering to adjust for differences between theatrical and home theatre listening environments.

Professional audio preparation should also address the consistency of levels between all sections of the program. A complex DVD title may contain dozens of video segments and menus, each with audio that may have been created or edited at different post-production studios around the world. A large level discrepancy between, for instance, the trailer audio and the menu audio, or between the main and commentary tracks in a feature film, forces consumers to adjust the volume control every time they jump to a different part of the disc. Instead, these volume adjustments should be addressed before the audio is encoded.

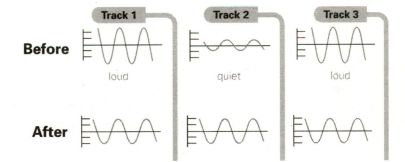

**Figure 7.8** Section-to-section levelling of the title's audio material ensures a consistent playback level throughout the program.

Another area of audio preparation that may be required for DVD is conforming, which means editing the audio tracks to be in sync with the video master. Especially when a movie has been out for several years or more, there may have been pull-ups or other changes made to picture elements without reference to sound elements. These changes may arise due to simply pulling out a damaged frame, or to making edits for specific venues such as airlines or broadcast. When an edited print is used as the master for encoding, the sound elements pulled for remixing may no longer be synchronized.

The potential for sync problems is compounded by DVD's ability to deliver multiple audio tracks in different languages. In the past, there may not have been a reason to ensure that the soundtracks in all of a film's release languages conform exactly to a given print of the picture. In DVD, the available French soundtrack might be taken from the film as it was released in France, while the English soundtrack is from the version released in Britain, where censorship might be more of an issue. The audio from each soundtrack used must be checked against and possibly conformed to the video version on the disc.

## Audio encoding

Even if the audio is destined for delivery in Dolby Digital or MPEG, the editing and enhancement steps outlined above always take place before encoding, while the audio is still in PCM. Once mixed and edited, the audio is ready to be encoded into the format that will be used on the DVD. If the audio is in mono or stereo, and is associated with a video program, it will most likely be delivered to the DVD facility on the audio tracks of the video source tape, which is hopefully in a format such as D1 or Digital Betacam that has good audio fidelity.

Multichannel programs, on the other hand, will be delivered on a separate tape that is striped with SMPTE time code for synchronization with the video material. The most widely used format for this application is MDM (Modular Digital Multi-track), usually referred to as (Tascam) DA-88. The DA-88 format accommodates up to eight channels on a single tape.

Professional DVD production systems allow the audio to be transferred from the source into the system in real time, with the encoding from PCM to Dolby Digital or MPEG taking place 'on-the-fly' in a single pass. Batch processing should be supported as well, allowing automated retrieval and capture.

If the DVD production facility is set up as a networked workgroup that includes an audio workstation (e.g. SonicStudio HD™ networked to DVD Creator) then audio tracks that have been mixed, edited, restored or otherwise enhanced on the audio station will not need to be captured into the authoring system from tape. Instead, the authoring tool can access the audio files over the network, and perform file-based encoding on any audio that needs to be compressed.

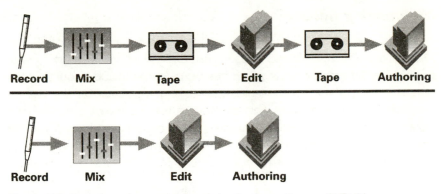

Record    Mix    Tape    Edit    Tape    Authoring

Record    Mix    Edit    Authoring

**Figure 7.9** Two alternative production chains for the audio on a DVD title.

Once captured, the audio needs to be thoroughly checked. Proper synchronization with the video source must be confirmed, as well as the absence of any artifacts (glitches or dropouts) introduced during the transfer. If surround material has been encoded to Dolby Digital, the audio operator will also need to compare decoded surround playback with the decoded down-mix in order to be sure that there is no phase cancellation or other problem. In addition, the material will also be checked at the various dynamic compression settings (not to be confused with data compression) supported by Dolby Digital, which allow the listener to set a consistently comfortable dialog level. A full-featured audio encoding environment for DVD will include monitoring modes that support all these types of listening evaluations.

# High-Density Audio™

As described earlier, both DVD-Audio and DVD-Video break new ground in audio fidelity by offering extremely high quality audio reproduction in formats designed for consumers. However, 16 bit stereo PCM at 44.1 or 48 kHz has been the norm for digital audio for many years, and the production infrastructure to support new audio capabilities is still developing. Therefore, while new formats will accelerate changes to conventional procedures, it is not yet clear what all of those changes will be. Even at this early stage, however, we can make some suggestions and observations about the practices and tools that will best support ultra-fidelity audio production in this new era.

## Maintaining fidelity

In general, audio with 20- or 24-bit resolution and a sample rate of 88.2 or 96 kHz (or higher) is referred to as High-Density Audio™. In working with this high-resolution audio, it is always best to capture the audio source in the highest resolution format available, and to keep the audio at the highest resolution as long as possible. This approach preserves the material with the highest fidelity for future use, while also preserving creative flexibility in the present.

High-resolution audio also requires very careful attention – in both the design of the audio equipment and the production practices employed – to guard against signal degradation as the material moves through various steps in the production chain. For example, sample-rate conversion can degrade audio quality when moving from high resolution to conventional resolution, particularly when a complex conversion (e.g. 96 to 44.1 kHz) is involved rather than a decimation (96 to 48 kHz). This problem can be minimized, however, by the use of appropriate quad-precision sample-rate conversion algorithms, and also by avoiding any unnecessary conversions during production.

Thus, in ensuring that high-resolution audio delivers on its potential, it is important that the right steps are taken at each and every stage of the audio handling chain. (Preserving the integrity of high-quality digital audio signals has been a long-standing concern of Sonic Solutions' co-founder, Dr Andy Moorer; the results of his work in this area have been incorporated into SonicStudio HD digital audio workstations.)

## Surround in film and music

With high-quality multichannel audio enabled on DVD-Audio (as well as DVD-Video), the already strong consumer interest in surround sound is likely to increase significantly in coming years. For the music industry, this phenomenon is one of the most striking differences introduced by the new audio formats.

Of course, the long-standing tradition of surround audio preparation in the film industry gives the recording business a head start in understanding some of the issues involved. Surround mixing techniques were pioneered for a variety of theatrical release formats as far back as the 1950s, and this tradition has been extended with the advent of home theatre systems and the extensive surround capabilities incorporated into DVD-Video.

It is important to understand, however, the very real differences between music and film applications of surround sound. Virtually all surround sound preparation and mixing techniques to date have been developed in a cinematic context. This means that:

- There is always a moving picture on which the attention of the audience is primarily focused.
- The audio program is 'synthetic,' created on the mixing stage from music, sound effects and dialog elements that never actually happened together in the 'real' world.
- The audio is meant to support dramatic action – to aid in the telling of the story. In most movies this means that dialog is the focal point.

The influence of these factors on film sound has led to the development of a surround mixing style in which dialog is commonly centred, music is mixed to the front left and right, and the surround channels are used mostly for ambience and perhaps occasional dramatic sound effects.

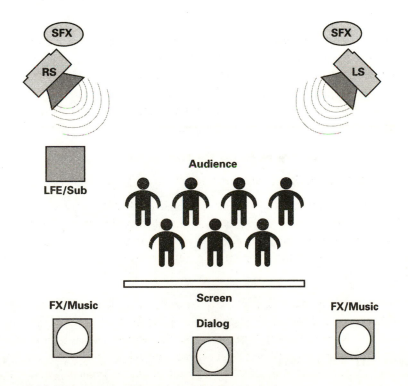

**Figure 7.10** Typical usage of channels in a 5.1 theatrical mix.

In contrast, music applications do not involve the support of on-screen action, and if there is any picture at all (e.g. stills on a DVD-Audio), the audio program is still the primary focus. Additionally, popular music recordings (other than live albums) generally do not attempt to present a realistic sound field that corresponds to a performance that happened or could have happened in a real place and time. So music will offer more freedom than film for experimentation with instrument placement in surround mixes. For now, it is too early to say whether the way surround sound is used in popular music will remain diverse or eventually become standardized (and if the latter, what the standard practices will be).

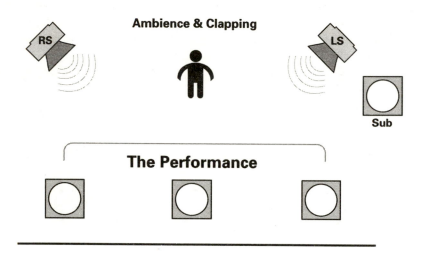

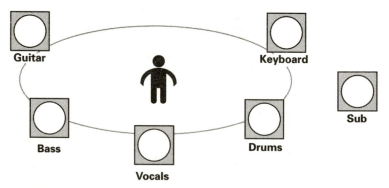

**Figure 7.11** Two approaches to channel usage in 5.1 channel surround mixing for music projects. The top diagram illustrates a typical audience perspective; the bottom puts the listener in the centre of the band.

## Performance recordings

The situation for recordings in fields such as classical music which involve the presentation of 'live' events — whether actual concerts or just 'real' instruments playing together in a studio — is quite different than for the typical studio album in popular music. The goal here is often to recreate a sense of the original sound in the room during the performance.

Dr Moorer has conducted some very interesting research in this area. Moorer started with a set of psycho-acoustic theorems originally proposed by Michael Gerzon, then tested their implications in a practical setting with assistance from the San Francisco Symphony and its chief recording engineer, Jack Vad. The details of this work are beyond the scope of this book. Amongst the more significant findings, however, are the following conclusions.

- An arrangement of three directional microphones provides as much signal information as any other microphone setup, even those using many microphones.
- Knowledge of the position and orientation of microphones used during a given recording may be used mathematically to derive an optimal reproduction of that recording through any size speaker array.
- The optimal mixing technique for any microphone array and any speaker placement can be shown to involve a combination of all signals in all speakers. In other words, recording a live event using an array of microphones placed in the same positions as the playback speakers may seem correct intuitively, but will not produce an optimal result.

It is Sonic's intent to incorporate the results of this work into future generations of SonicStudio HD systems designed for High-Density Audio™ (high-resolution) surround sound pre-mastering. The coming years will no doubt see the professional audio industry in general continuing to evolve new tools and techniques for the reproduction of music in surround settings.

## Multi-format production

Traditionally, audio workstations assume that at any given moment, the user is working on a single program designed for a single venue; DVD challenges that assumption. In particular, when multiple versions — stereo and multichannel, for example — are intended to represent the same program, it may be important to ensure that editing and sonic enhancement is applied consistently to both programs.

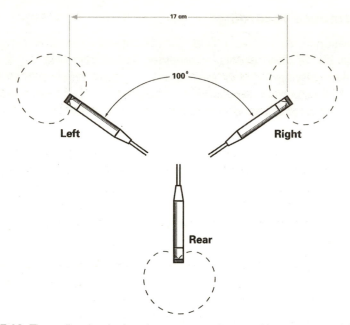

**Figure 7.12** Three directional microphones arranged to provide accurate spatial information for multichannel recording.

Professional editors and mixers will want to be able to quickly and seamlessly switch between a high-resolution multichannel version, a high-resolution stereo version, and a standard-resolution stereo version, checking that imaging, balance and levels are consistent and that nothing of interest has inadvertently been left or processed out.

Of particular interest will be the compatibility in a given mix between multichannel and stereo modes. In a five-channel recording with the vocalist at centre, for instance, it will be crucial for the mixer to check whether the centre channel program is out of phase with the left and right front channels, and to see what happens when these channels are collapsed into a stereo mix.

## Still images and subpictures

While presentation of time-based content (motion video and audio) is the main focus in both DVD-Video and DVD-Audio, still images are also an integral part of these formats. The use of stills encompasses several distinct roles: still pictures are used for slide shows and still shows, as menu backgrounds, and as subpictures.

In menus, subpictures are overlayed on the background images to give user feedback (highlights) for selected menu choices. During program playback, subpicture overlays are used to display subtitles (up to 32 subtitle streams are available for multiple languages) and other synchronized text, such as lyrics.

In DVD's subpicture system, the player can display up to four different colours at a time overlayed on the main image (the menu background, or the video program that is being subtitled). The area(s) of the screen in which each of these colours is displayed is defined by a mask that is prepared as a separate single-colour bitmap graphic (no anti-aliasing or gradients allowed).

The colour used in each of the four masks is not the colour that the player will actually display in the defined areas. Instead, the mask colours are defined in the DVD specification: white for 'Background' areas, black for 'Pattern' areas (generally basic text or graphics), and red and blue for 'Emphasis' (additional text or graphic elements).

During playback, the player uses the four masks to determine where the background, pattern and emphasis areas are on the screen. Each area is mapped to a display colour drawn from a 16-colour palette defined in the current Program Chain. The transparency level of each colour is defined in authoring (the background colour usually has a transparency value of 0 per cent, allowing the underlying image to show through).

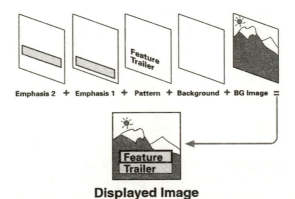

Emphasis 2 **+** Emphasis 1 **+** Pattern **+** Background **+** BG Image **=**

**Displayed Image**

**Figure 7.13** DVD's subpicture overlay system composites four overlay layers and a background image to create the displayed picture.

On menus, subpicture colour mapping is defined for each of three states. The normal state maps the subpicture masks for areas of the screen that are outside of any button highlight areas (hot spots), or inside the highlight areas of buttons that are not currently selected. The selected state maps colours for areas inside the hot spot of the currently selected button. The activated state defines the colour mapping inside of the hot spot when a button is activated.

Both menu overlay graphics and still images are originally created as bitmaps in formats such as .TIFF or .PICT, normally using an image editing application such as Adobe Photoshop®. The still images are created in full 24-bit colour, and then individually compressed as MPEG-2 I-pictures.

In the case of subtitle overlays, the first step is to create a script showing the text to be displayed and the timecode information that will be used to synchronize the display with the source video. This script is then converted to a series of bitmap graphic images that are imported into the DVD production application along with the associated timecode information. The preparation of subtitling is often handled by specialized subtitling service bureaus.

## Menu graphics for video

Because a viewer's experience of a DVD title is largely defined by the menus used to access content, menu design is a crucial aspect of asset preparation. The navigational flow-chart for a title is defined in the project planning stage, and perhaps the general look and feel of the menus as well. But it is during the asset preparation stage that the menu designs are brought to life and finalized.

The appropriate approach to menu design for a given title will be determined by both the amount and the character of the title's content. Some titles will use a minimal approach which makes access to the content as direct as possible. In other titles the menus are intended to be content in their own right, giving users an engaging interactive experience that sets the tone for the main content.

Because interactive design has been an important element of CD-ROM production for over a decade, DVD menu design is often handled by designers from the world of computer-based multimedia. It is important to realize, however, that DVD (meaning DVD-Video and DVD-Audio) is a video platform, not a computer platform. This means that graphics and menus need to be designed with the specific characteristics of television-based video in mind.

One important difference between the computer space and the TV space is in colour palettes. The range of colours supported in the NTSC and PAL colour space is different from those supported in the RGB (red, green, blue) world of computer displays. Designers need to take into account how their colour choices will translate when displayed on a TV screen.

Another consideration is correctly matching the size of the graphics with the aspect ratio and format of the video program. This is complicated by the fact that the graphics are normally prepared on computers, but they must look correct on televisions. Computer displays and graphic design tools use square pixels, while television displays use rectangular pixels that are about 10 per cent taller than they are wide. Thus, a 720 × 540 image yields a 4 : 3 aspect ratio on a computer, but a 720 × 480 image yields a 4 : 3 aspect ratio on a television.

If the aspect ratio of a DVD's video material is 4 : 3, graphics for static and motion menus should be prepared at a resolution of 720 × 540 pixels, then scaled before being imported into the DVD authoring tool. The scaled resolution will be 720 × 480 for NTSC, and 720 × 576 for PAL. This will make the graphics look vertically stretched or compressed on the computer display (depending on whether they are scaled for NTSC or PAL), but when the graphic is ultimately displayed on a video monitor, the image will be correctly proportioned.

If, on the other hand, the aspect ratio for the DVD is 16 : 9, menus are prepared at 960 × 540, then scaled to 720 × 480 (NTSC) or 720 × 576 (PAL). The scaled graphics will look vertically compressed on a computer, but will appear at the proper aspect ratio when displayed on a widescreen (16 : 9) television.

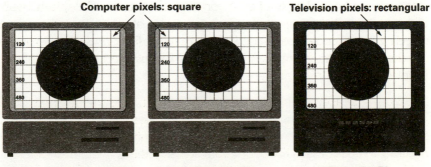

**Figure 7.14** Menu backgrounds prepared in a computer graphics environment are scaled to compensate for the rectangular pixels used in television.

Within these resolutions for each type of menu, designers also need to be aware of the 'safe area'. In computer graphics, an image in a given resolution is displayed in its entirety on screen. But when the same image is displayed on a television, the outer 5–10 per cent of the image may not be visible. These outer edges are referred to as being outside the safe area. Menu design for television will take this into account by not placing any crucial text, icons or selection areas outside of the safe area.

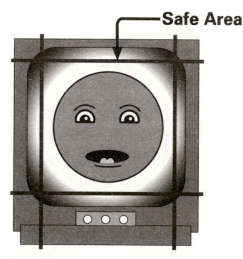

**Figure 7.15** The 'safe area' on a television monitor.

Finally, the definition of images displayed on computer monitors is far greater than that of the same size image displayed on television. This means that text which appears crisp and clear on a computer display (progressive scan) may be barely legible (if at all) on television. Text for television needs to be bigger and bolder, which means that less of it will fit on any given screen. Fonts that are comprised of single pixel lines or serifs should be avoided because they tend to flicker in the NTSC playback environment due to interlaced scan.

The many potential complications involved in menu preparation underscore the necessity of budgeting production time for thorough checking of menu assets prior to importing them into the DVD production tool. Double-checking the basics such as spelling, safe areas, legibility, and button/highlight alignment will avoid problems later, helping to keep a project on track as it moves through the authoring phase of DVD production.

# Chapter 8

# Authoring

The concept of authoring comes from the field of interactive multimedia. In essence, authoring is a media integration process, where individual media elements – audio, video, graphics and text – are combined into a unified whole, with navigational pathways linking the various parts. The greater the number of individual elements, and the more flexible the navigation between parts (the interactivity), the more complex the authoring task.

For consumer audio and video devices, the need to author material for release in a given format is pretty much a new concept, which makes authoring potentially the least-understood stage in pre-mastering for video and audio professionals. With VHS, for instance, there is no need (or capability) whatever to program logic into the video or audio content itself. The only interactivity (such as it is) involved in VHS playback comes entirely from the logic of transport controls (play, rewind, etc.) on the player itself.

CD-Audio is a little less linear than VHS, because the format supports navigation directly to track and index points, and the listener may select modes (shuffle, for instance) which vary the playback order. In traditional CD production, the analogous process to authoring is the planning and insertion (PQ coding) of these track and index marks. Still, CDs are hardly considered interactive, and viewed in the context of the overall work that goes into a CD-Audio release, PQ coding is a very minor step.

With the new DVD-based formats, authoring can be significantly more involved. Preparing video, audio and graphical assets does not by itself create a DVD, it merely readies the assets for the authoring process. The question of how involved that process will be depends on the project template or flowchart developed in the planning stage, because authoring is largely the process of bringing that template to life.

As we learned earlier, a DVD-Video or DVD-Audio title is conceptually made up of two basic types of information: presentation data (video, audio, graphics) stored in VOBs and AOBs; and navigation data (the playback conditions and instructions called Program Chains) that define how and when to play back the presentation data. Authoring is largely the process of creating PGCs and the VOBs or AOBs that they reference.

Specifically, DVD authoring may involve tying together encoded audio and video streams, laying out multiple audio tracks or angles, importing or generating subtitles, and defining chapter points, button behaviours and the navigational interface. Authoring is also where special features such as parental block, language codes, region codes and copy protection are enabled.

Of course, many of these tasks do not apply to Pure Audio DVD-Audio titles. Depending on the format and the included project elements, then, we see two distinct paths for the authoring of DVD titles.

# Pure Audio titles

The simplest case covers Pure Audio DVD-Audio titles. The audio elements will be edited, sequenced, assembled, and pre-mastered (adjusted for levels and enhanced with EQ (equalization) and dynamics processing) in an audio-centric environment, such as SonicStudio HD, which supports both stereo and surround. Track and Index information will then be added, and Real Time Text elements (if any) will be synchronized to audio. All elements, along with an authoring script, will then be transferred to a format server, where multiplexed streams and files will be generated to produce a finished disc image.

# DVD-Video and Audio-with-Video

While each format is governed by its own distinct specification, a full-featured DVD-Audio title includes not just high-resolution audio, but also all the visual elements (graphics, menus and video) that one finds on a DVD-Video title. Because of this, the authoring processes for these two formats

Interactive/Video Authoring

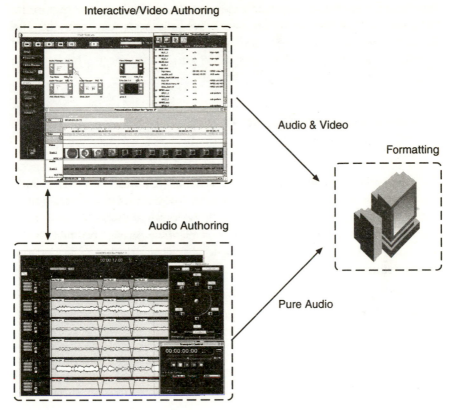

Audio & Video

Formatting

Audio Authoring

Pure Audio

**Figure 8.1** The authoring process may involve both visual and audio production environments.

are very similar, while following a very different path from that of a Pure Audio title. For convenience, we will look at these similar processes together.

The process of creating a multimedia DVD title may proceed in parallel (more than one task occurring simultaneously) if the authoring system allows assets to be represented by containers or placeholders that are filled later with the actual content. However, for the sake of clarity, we will treat DVD-Video/Audio-with-Video authoring as if it were a series of sequential steps.

As with a Pure Audio title, the audio program elements in an Audio-with-Video title will be prepared in an audio-centric editing and pre-mastering environment. Video and graphical elements, meanwhile, will be prepared and encoded as described earlier.

After asset preparation, the media elements, together with any text in the title, will be transferred to an interactive authoring environment. The elements will be combined and their interrelationships defined, and eventually the program will be formatted into a final image. The following steps are generally involved in this process:

## Storyboarding/title layout

Storyboarding is really another way of referring to the project planning phase that we discussed earlier. It is included here because an advanced DVD production system (such as Sonic DVD Creator AV) will include project planning aids such as templates, built-in assistants, and bit budgeting. In this kind of authoring environment, it becomes possible to develop a storyboard for the title during the project planning phase, and then to use that same storyboard directly as a skeletal framework that is fleshed out during authoring.

Alternatively, storyboarding may be done manually. However it is accomplished, it is absolutely·crucial that a project be thoroughly thought out and documented as early as possible in the production process.

The storyboard shows all of the assets (even if they have not yet been captured or assembled) and all of the menus and navigational links that will join the assets together into a seamless title. It serves three main purposes:

- To provide a roadmap for multiple operators working on the same project, avoiding errors in asset assembly and menu creation.
- As a checklist for the producer to ensure that production resources are allocated appropriately and to minimize rework.
- As a 'pre-flight check' of the title's navigation in order to avoid dead ends, confusing or overly-complicated menus, or inconsistent and user-unfriendly disc navigation.

Amongst the project parameters that a storyboard will help to define are the size of the disc (DVD-5, DVD-9, DVD-10, DVD-18), the number of audio streams, the video content (including multiple angles, if any), and information such as region coding and parental blocking (for DVD-Video). The end result of the process will be a complete roadmap of the DVD title, as well as a Bit Budget and asset list.

To facilitate storyboarding before asset preparation, it is useful to lay out projects using placeholder icons that can later be assigned to audio,

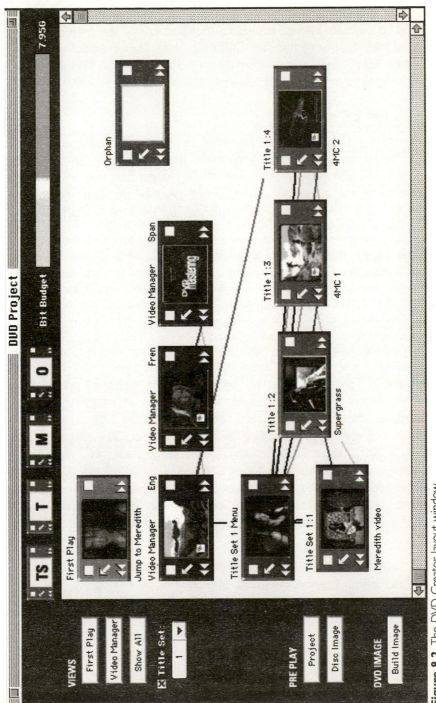

**Figure 8.2** The DVD Creator layout window.

video, or menus. As assets are imported, the total number of bits used should be carefully tracked to ensure that the size of the project will not exceed the capacity of the disc. DVD Creator's layout window is shown in Figure 8.2.

## Assembly of assets

The next step is to import and assemble all of the prepared source assets: video, audio, menu graphics, subpictures, and subtitles. In an integrated production environment, many of these assets will be immediately accessible to the authoring station, either because the same machine is used for both preparation and authoring, or because a workgroup of machines is networked together.

At this stage, encoded video and audio files will likely already be in the form needed for DVD, while graphics files in bitmap formats will need to be converted to MPEG stills. Advanced authoring environments will allow file import, including automatic bitmap conversion, to be handled with a simple drag-and-drop interface.

Even greater efficiency may be achieved in a networked production environment that supports batch encoding, multiplexing and formatting of assets. In Sonic DVD Creator, for instance, the authoring process may proceed entirely without any source assets. When all authoring decisions are made, the resultant project template may be used to drive a network of encoding, formatting and DVD-R and DLT (Digital Linear Tape) writing stations. This network-based automation process, handled by the AutoSonic Server, can speed DVD production by placing the bulk of the decisions in the authoring and template creation steps. Once a project is dispatched to the AutoSonic Server, the author may begin working on a new project while encoding for the first one proceeds automatically.

In a traditional workflow, once the elementary media files are imported, they are linked together to build objects (VOBs or AOBs). The basic media type of the object (video for VOBs and audio for AOBs), may appear in the authoring environment on a timeline, against which additional streams – the audio and subtitle streams of a VOB, for instance, or the still pictures in an AOB slide show – can be laid in. These elemental streams are not yet multiplexed (interleaved) together, however, allowing the author freely to modify the way in which the assets are assembled as the project evolves.

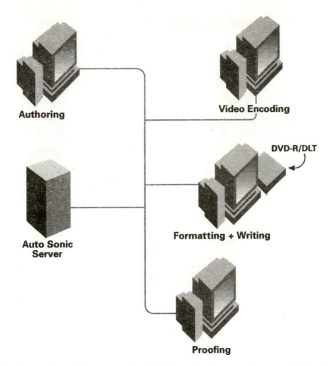

**Figure 8.3** Network architecture of a DVD production workgroup utilizing the AutoSonic Server.

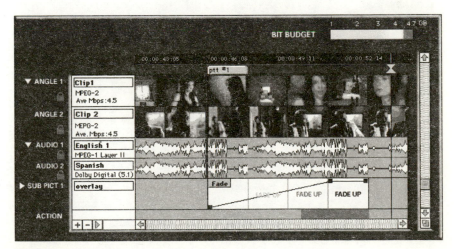

**Figure 8.4** The DVD Creator presentation window.

## Defining menus and buttons

Once stills for menus are imported, it is possible to define highlight areas, specify highlight colours, and create 'hot spots' for buttons, determining which areas of the screen may be selected and activated with the remote control (or a mouse during computer-hosted playback). Depending on the number of menus, and the buttons on each, this may be one of the most labour-intensive aspects of authoring a title. It is essential for the authoring tool to provide a graphical interface for subpicture assembly that allows fast, intuitive control of features such as button activation times and highlights.

## Defining interactivity

Once the objects have been assembled and menus laid out, it is time to create Program Chains to give the title interactivity. DVD-Video, in particular, supports sophisticated use of jumps, links, conditional branching and other navigational devices that have applications in gaming and training.

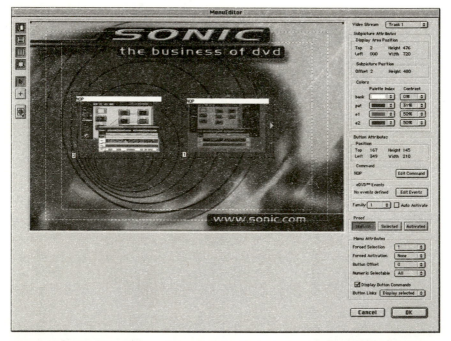

**Figure 8.5** The Menu Editor window in Sonic DVD Creator is used to define button highlights and hot spots.

However, even a simple menu-driven DVD requires a set of instructions that determines what happens when the user activates a given menu button.

As part of defining interactivity, the pre- and post-commands (if any) for the various PGCs are set, and connections are made between the PGCs and the presentation data to which they refer (the title's Audio Object Sets and/or Video Object Sets).

## *Proofing*

Because of the constant interplay amongst the audio, video and interactive elements throughout the authoring process, it must be possible at any time for the author and producer to preview or proof the project as it will behave in the player. This preview capability should permit the project to be seen and heard at full resolution, and should fully support the checking of interactivity to avoid surprises. That will allow the production team to spot encoding artifacts or other problems in the elemental media, and to test the interactive design for ease and clarity. By facilitating constant revision and improvement, accurate proofing is an essential ingredient of professional title production.

**Figure 8.6** Built-in proofing controls allow the author to check the project at any time to ensure that it plays back with the expected media quality and navigational behaviour.

## Defining eDVD™ links

If the title is an eDVD™ — a Web-enhanced hybrid disc designed to play DVD-Video content from a browser when played in a DVD-ROM drive — the DVD authoring process will include defining relationships between HTML pages and DVD-Video material. As the project is authored, URLs and browser frames may be directly linked with menu buttons and specific points in the video timeline. A mouse-over on a DVD menu, for example, may be set up to trigger multiple browser events, or to jump to a new URL in any target window.

**Figure 8.7** The eDVD module in Sonic DVD Creator and DVD Fusion allows the author to define links between HTML pages and DVD-Video content.

When title authoring is complete, the Sonic eDVD engine automatically creates an eDVD player application which is written to the DVD-ROM section of the DVD title. The eDVD player runs on top of a personal computer's pre-existing DVD player, and serves as the video and web interface for the eDVD title. When installed, the eDVD player gives viewers instant access to any of the HTTP links in the DVD title, as well as a simple and straightforward DVD player interface for viewing the standard DVD content.

## Formatting/multiplexing

When the cycle of authoring and proofing yields an approved title, the project is readied for output. The presentation data (audio, video, subpictures) are multiplexed together into AOBs and/or VOBs. The PGCs are incorporated into the AMGI (the Audio Manager Information area), the VMGI (the Video Manager Information area), or the VTSIs (the Video Title Set Information areas at the beginning of each VTS). Additionally, the volume information (for titles with multiple volumes spread across multiple discs or sides) is generated. The end result is a new set of files which comply with the DVD-Video or DVD-Audio format specification.

Based on the decisions and definitions made in the authoring stage, the formatting process is completely deterministic. Once initiated, it requires no further input or supervision.

Sophisticated multiplexing technologies, such as Sonic's HyperMux™, for example, optimize performance based on an analysis of the title's interaction and data. This approach, however, is computationally intensive and requires back-and-forth access to the complete project. The authoring system may be isolated from this burden with a 'format server' configuration, in which the server resides on a separate, network-connected computer. The authoring environment passes an authoring script and an asset list to the format server, which then analyses, multiplexes and assembles the logical image. In an AutoSonic automated DVD production network, the format server can be driven remotely by the authoring tools and can batch-multiplex multiple jobs.

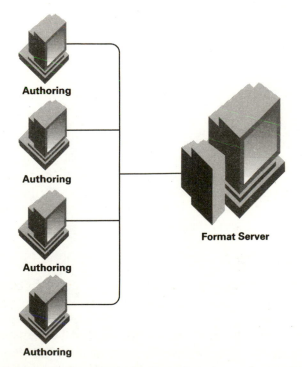

**Figure 8.8** Architecture of a networked system using a remote format server to format projects from multiple authoring stations.

If a Sonic Solutions authoring package is being used to create the disc image, the user will also have the option at this stage of outputting the DVD title as an sDVD, a DVD stream that has been data-compressed for delivery over a broadband Internet connection, intranet, or other network. When sDVD output is selected, all source video is automatically compressed into low bit-rate MPEG-2 video. Once compressed, the video and audio assets are multiplexed into a file consistent in structure with the DVD-Video file format. This file may be written to hard disk, and also to the DVD-ROM portion of a standard DVD-Video title.

Another multiplexing and formatting option available with Sonic Solutions tools will be to create an hDVD title playable on DVD-ROM equipped computers (hDVD-capable DVD software is required for playback). hDVDs combine the features of the DVD-Video format with the resolution and quality of High Definition Digital TV.

## Creating the disc image

The next step is to create the disc image. If the title will be replicated, the copy protection flags are set so that the data can be encrypted by the manufacturing plant as the discs are glass-mastered. The logical image files are formatted for the UDF file system and written to the delivery medium. Once again, this process may be automated, as in an AutoSonic production network.

The delivery medium used depends on the application. For replication of discs at a DVD plant, the currently accepted standard premastering format is a 20 GB DLT. Developments in alternative optical and magnetic formats continue, and the possibility also exists to send a DVD disc image to a plant over a network. While these factors will likely influence the form in which DVD plants accept masters in the future, for now DLT remains the standard delivery medium for DVD replication.

Projects requiring only a one-off disc, meanwhile, are generally written to DVD-Recordable (DVD-R). It may also be less expensive to duplicate discs (record copies) onto DVD-R than to have discs replicated when only very small quantities of discs are required.

Since 4.7 GB DVD-R drives and media became available in mid-1999, DVD-R has been a viable format for one-offs requiring the full capacity of a DVD-5, potentially allowing a DVD-R to serve as a master for a DVD-5 (or two DVD-Rs for two sides of a DVD-10). With the cost of the drives down to less than a third of their original price (and continuing to drop), DVD-R is also now within reach of a broader class of title developers.

If the total data used by a DVD title is less than 650 MB, the content may alternatively be output and delivered as a cDVD, an extension to the DVD format which allows a CD-ROM to be formatted as a DVD and read on a computer with a CD-ROM drive (or a DVD-ROM drive).

In order to read a cDVD, the playback computer uses a software-based cDVD player, which is automatically embedded in the DVD-Others zone of a cDVD by authoring tools from Sonic Solutions. cDVDs are not currently playable on set-top DVD-Video players. The cDVD disc image would normally be output to CD-R, either for direct use or for delivery to the CD replication plant as a cDVD master.

## Pre-replication QC

While not currently accepted at all replication plants, DVD-R and rewritable DVD formats can still play an important role in the authoring process for DVDs that will ultimately be delivered to the plant on DLT. This is because they can be very useful for pre-replication quality control of a DVD disc image.

Once a DVD disc image has been generated, it should once again be proofed for audio and video quality, audio/video sync, and navigation. By playing back the disc image prior to replication, the producer gets a preview of what the finished title will look like when it is played by the end-user on a set-top DVD player. This final quality check is an opportunity to catch problems without waiting for a check-disc from the replication plant.

For titles that will be replicated as DVD-5s, DVD-R has been a valuable tool for pre-replication testing, particularly since its capacity increased to 4.7 GB. Widely compatible, DVD-Rs are used for testing title performance both in computer-hosted DVD-ROM drives and in DVD-Video players.

Another option for proofing disc images is the DVD-RAM format, available since mid-1998. Much less expensive than DVD-R, DVD-RAM fits well with the expansion of DVD authoring capabilities into smaller-scale operations with lower budgets. However, the format has so far been of limited use for title testing because of its 2.6-GB per side capacity. Version 2, however, boosts single-sided capacity to 4.7 GB (to be followed by support for 9.4 GB double-sided discs). The new version began shipping in limited quantities in December of 1999, and became widely available in mid-2000.

With Version 2, a 4.7-GB single-sided DVD-RAM disc is playable not only in a DVD-RAM drive, but also in DVD-RAM-capable DVD-ROM drives, which came to the market in late 1999. The same discs will also play in DVD-RAM-capable DVD-Video players, which have been available since mid-2000. These developments mean that DVD-RAM offers title developers an affordable, rewritable medium for both desktop and set-top testing.

As for other rewritable formats, the capacity of the DVD-RW format (Book F of the DVD specification) is also specified at 4.7 GB, and the development of 4.7 GB capacity for DVD+RW (not part of the DVD specification) has been announced. As of this writing, however, these formats were not yet on the market. It is also important to recognize that none of the 4.7 GB recordables (DVD-R) or rewritables (DVD-RAM, DVD-RW, DVD+RW) will fully address pre-replication proofing needs for dual-layer discs such as DVD-9 and DVD-18.

## *Disc manufacturing and testing*

Once the disc image is approved, the pre-mastering tape is sent to the replication plant. The image is loaded onto the hard disk of the mastering

**Figure 8.9** A DVD replication system used to mass-produce DVD discs.

system, the encryption flags set during authoring are evaluated, and the program data are encrypted accordingly. A glass master is cut from the data, stampers are derived from the master, and discs are injection-moulded from the stampers. The discs are then metalized, bonded, coated, printed and packaged. Ideally, samples from this production run will be thoroughly tested in a number of different player models and drives before the finished product is shipped to distributors.

# Chapter 9

# Production environment and workflow

So far, we've covered the steps in the DVD production process, but we haven't really looked at how those steps are most effectively accomplished. It won't help much to fall back on workflow models from existing video and audio formats. Traditionally, even in delivery media where sound and picture are presented together (film, television, home video), the production work on audio is mostly handled separately from work on the picture, with integration into a single medium taking place at the final stages. The two crafts have developed in parallel but independently, with little sharing of resources, standards, operating procedures, or personnel.

This approach seems to work well in film and television, and it may also be fine for the upstream production work often involved in making a DVD, such as shooting and editing a video featurette, or recording audio commentary tracks. But the fact that DVD-Video and DVD-Audio are integrated formats, where every element on a disc potentially influences every other (remember the Bit-Budget™), argues strongly for an integrated workflow where every element is easily accessible at every production stage. Collections of inflexible single-purpose 'black boxes' – first-generation DVD tools with little potential for central control or information sharing – are ill-adapted to the demands of an integrated process, and will lead to bottlenecks and inefficiencies.

# Integrated production environment

The alternative to the first-generation approach is an integrated production environment. The incorporation of asset preparation, authoring, proofing and imaging all into a unified environment removes barriers to the iterative cycle of proofing and revision, on which quality title production depends. Elements can be easily imported – and updated elements re-imported – directly from files created by asset preparation tools in the same system, without time-consuming transfers. An integrated environment also enables a system such as AutoSonic™ to batch-encode source assets directly from their stored locations throughout a production network.

Because DVD and its associated technologies have applications in so many different areas, there is no one 'right' way to set up an integrated production facility. Within the integrated work model, there are several main variants: the all-in-one, standalone workstation, an integrated NLE/DVD publishing environment, and a multi-user networked workgroup.

# Questions to ask

Before deciding which approach to DVD production makes the most sense for your situation, it is important to define the type of work you expect to

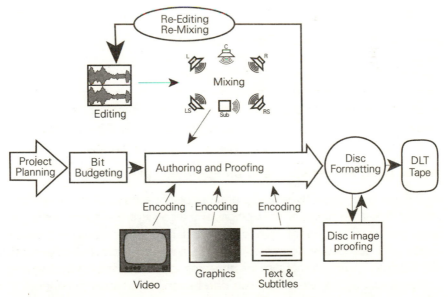

**Figure 9.1** Workflow of an integrated DVD production environment.

accomplish, and under what conditions. Once again, thinking through the answers to a set of questions is a good way to start.

## In what areas will your DVD activities be concentrated?

With versatility being one of the defining attributes of DVD, it is no surprise that applications for the format may be found in many different fields, including film, music, advertising, video post, corporate communications, and multimedia gaming. But while DVDs are used in all these areas, a feature film title for home video is quite different from a title for a museum kiosk. These differences are reflected in the different ways that production of titles in various fields is organized. To optimize your workflow, it is very important to start with a clear idea of the types of clients you expect to serve, or – if the 'client' happens to be you or others within your own organization – what category of client you fall into.

### Home video and recorded music

One of the main distinctions between the different types of markets in which DVD is used is whether the titles are mass-produced for commercial distribution to consumers or used for internal purposes. The clearest example of the former is currently the home video market, but many of the same workflow considerations may be expected to apply to producing music titles when DVD-Audio is available.

The commercial realities of these market segments dictate a workflow designed to output titles with both the highest-possible production values (video and audio fidelity) and the highest-possible throughput. Optimal productivity is achieved in networked, multi-user settings that allow production to proceed in parallel, with operators concentrating on creative work while automated processing tasks are handled in the background.

### Video post, advertising, and independent production

DVD's utility for delivery of video content goes beyond just the home video market. For showing a portfolio or pitching a concept, the format offers an attractive combination of high quality and random-access convenience. Video post-production houses, for instance, are finding that many clients are attracted to DVD as a medium for obtaining approvals, delivering programs to reviewers, and other limited-run distribution tasks currently handled by VHS dubs. The same is true for independent producers, for whom DVD publishing is a new service to offer to clients. In advertising, meanwhile, DVD is becoming the preferred source for viewing video content, and video producers working in advertising are finding that it is rapidly becoming critical to be able to publish on DVD.

In these video-centric industries, where DVD production is not the main focus, the addition of DVD capabilities is most efficient when systems are designed to fit seamlessly with the existing production workflow. For instance, when DVD functionality is integrated with the NLE systems commonly used for editing in video post houses and ad agencies, edited video files may be transcoded directly to MPEG-2 video, without first being transferred to tape for capture/encoding.

## Corporate and institutional

Corporate AV departments are finding numerous uses for DVD, including presentations, trade-show displays, employee and/or customer training, and point-of-sale kiosks. Similar applications are found at museums, libraries and educational institutions.

The source materials used in these fields is diverse. If the primary focus is on video, an NLE system may already be present, and an approach similar to the video post workflow may work well. On the other hand, many projects are more multimedia oriented, with quizzes, several languages and web links in addition to multiple video clips. Such titles often involve greater interactive complexity than linear video presentations, and the organization of production may well reflect an emphasis on flexibility and customization rather than standardization and throughput.

## Multimedia publishing

The diversity and interactivity found in much corporate DVD work also applies to commercially published multimedia DVD, which ranges from games to reference and information titles. The workflow may be similar to that found at developers of multimedia CD-ROM, but with tools supporting the DVD specification and optimized for DVD media types and navigation.

## Videographers and enthusiasts

With DVD player penetration growing rapidly in consumer households, the format is becoming increasingly attractive as a video delivery medium for both professional event videographers and video enthusiasts. This trend will likely accelerate with the proliferation of Digital Video camcorders, the enhanced video-handling capabilities of personal computers, and the improved capacity and compatibility of inexpensive, writeable DVD formats such as DVD-RAM, DVD-R, and DVD+RW.

While consumers will want to see events in their own lives – weddings, anniversaries, birthday parties – on Hollywood-like DVDs, it is unlikely the demand will be high for complex interactivity. Thus the highest priorities in DVD publishing for this market will likely be simplicity and fast turnaround.

## What are the typical types of DVD titles to be produced for your target market?

DVD's versatility allows for a great diversity of title types, and new genres of DVD are likely to emerge as the format matures. Most titles, however, fall into one of several general categories described below. It is important to keep in mind while planning your facility which of these types of DVDs your clients will be asking you to make, and what is involved in making them. Remember as well that any title in the DVD-Video or DVD-Audio format may include additional information or capabilities – a database, computer game or Web connection, for instance – that are available to the user when the disc is played from a computer-hosted DVD-ROM drive.

### Feature-length DVD movies

These titles typically contain more than 60 minutes of video material, generally one main program with perhaps one or more associated 'featurettes.' For instance, a 90-minute feature film might be accompanied by a 20-minute 'The Making of...' short subject. The emphasis is normally on linear presentation of the video programs, with minimal navigational options within each program. Designed for playback on DVD-Video set-top players, such titles must be compliant with the DVD-Video specification. Because of the length of the video material, VBR encoding capability will be required.

At the premium end of the home video market, movie titles now commonly include additional value-added features such as immersive 3D menus, side-by-side comparison of storyboards with finished scenes, or links between the shooting script and the feature presentation. When played

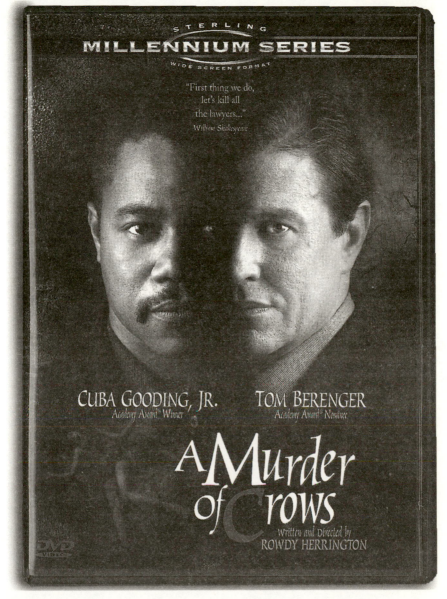

**Figure 9.2** A feature film DVD-Video title. (Images courtesy of Sterling Home Entertainment, LLC. Copyright © 2000 by Sterling Home Entertainment, LLC)

in DVD-ROM drives, these titles often include direct links to a promotional Web site which includes merchandising and special activities such as contests. Thus, title production for home video is a considerably more complex field today than it was just two years ago.

## DVD-Audio music albums

As we saw earlier, DVD-Audio is a very flexible format that allows for inclusion of a wide variety of extra media such as slide shows, lyrics, music videos, and documentary video. As with home video titles, DVD-Audio releases will probably also be Web-connected, linking fans to the band or label site for tour information, contests and merchandise.

As of this writing, it is too early to say exactly how producers and record labels will choose to use DVD-Audio's capabilities, and what consumers will expect. We do know, however, that a DVD-Audio production facility will need, at a minimum, the capability to enhance and prepare high-resolution audio formats in both stereo and multichannel configurations. Beyond that, audio mastering facilities may choose to hand off the multimedia aspects of their projects to existing facilities that also handle DVD-Video, or they may take the opportunity to extend their own reach into new markets.

## Music video and karaoke

While DVD-Audio is new, music applications of DVD-Video are not. The existence of many successful 'in concert' music video titles, as well as DVD's ideal characteristics for both music video compilations and karaoke, mean that music is often cited as the second most popular category of commercially available DVD-Video titles (after feature films).

Audio quality is clearly a priority in music DVD-Video titles, which may take advantage of the format's PCM capabilities to deliver CD-quality (or better) sound. Except for concert videos, music video and karaoke titles will normally contain multiple short video clips. In addition to menu-based navigation, such titles may also be authored automatically to play through the clips, like tracks on an audio CD. Karaoke titles will include at least two audio streams: one with lead vocals and another without, and may take advantage of the multiple 'karaoke down-mix' modes within the Dolby Digital format.

## Presentations and kiosks

The availability of both industrial DVD-Video players and DVD-enabled laptops has made DVD the ideal medium for many corporate and institutional multimedia presentations formerly delivered on LaserDisc, videotape or directly from the hard drive of a laptop computer. DVD is perfect for integrated presentations combining bullet points with top-quality

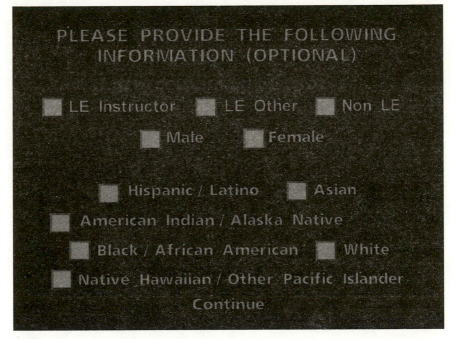

**Figure 9.3** An information-gathering screen from a DVD-Video based kiosk. (Courtesy of Zuma Digital)

video, and the format's navigational capabilities allow presentations to be easily tailored on-the-fly for a given audience. With a DVD laptop, non-technical executive or sales personnel can deliver such presentations in any venue, from a shareholder's meeting to a one-on-one with an important client.

Using an industrial player, DVD-Video content may be synchronized with lighting, live sound and other presentation media for a tightly-integrated production. At the same time, industrial players allow unattended playback to be scheduled at predetermined times in settings such as trade shows, museums and point-of-purchase. Industrial players are also well suited for touch-screen-based kiosks with applications in museums, retailing and public facilities.

## Interactive DVD

Titles that make extensive use of the interactive capabilities of DVD (primarily DVD-Video) may range from learning titles (education and training) to games. In general, titles will be structured to take advantage of the format's strengths (image and sound quality), using multiple short video and audio clips with a navigational structure that involves the end user in determining the order of playback, either directly through menus or on-the-fly through user input during playback.

The DVD-Video specification provides General parameter locations for the storing of user responses, allowing conditional navigation based, for instance, on keeping track of a user's score in a game. However, title design will have to take into account that memory is limited compared to PC-based interactive platforms, and that playback performance is not optimized for action games.

The navigational complexity of interactive titles accentuates the importance of authoring in the title preparation process, and places increased demands on the project planning, interface design, proofing and quality control phases of production. Many interactive titles will probably take advantage of DVD-Video's ability to switch seamlessly between multiple angles at playback, thereby adding to the video material to be captured and stored on the disc, and increasing the likelihood of VBR encoding.

## Pure DVD-ROM

While the title types above may be hybrids that include DVD-ROM information in the DVD-Others zone, they are designed primarily for playback on set-top DVD players. A pure DVD-ROM title has no DVD-Video or DVD-Audio zone, and thus will play only on a computer-hosted DVD-ROM drive. These titles typically deliver much the same information as found on CD-ROM, but take advantage of DVD's massive capacity. DVD-ROM data may include text and word processing documents, database and spreadsheet files, multimedia presentations, digital audio, graphics and video, HTML pages, and browsers supporting Web connectivity.

## Web-connected hybrid (eDVD™)

With eDVD™, the DVD-Video content on a title is enhanced by integrating it into a Web-connected browser when it is played on a DVD-ROM equipped computer. DVD titles in many of the categories above – feature film, music, corporate, gaming – can benefit greatly from the addition of Web connectivity. Links to the Web may be used to enable commerce and merchandising, provide documentation and updated information, facilitate individualized learning or training, and draw users into chats, contests and other 'community' activities.

In addition to the general production considerations involved with a title in a given category, adding Web connectivity will normally involve the close coordination of production efforts for the DVD-Video material and the Web material. Web design expertise (in-house or outsourced) will likely be necessary to ensure effective integration of these two mediums.

**Figure 9.4** Sonic's eDVD is an example of Web-connected DVD technology. Using industry-standard Interactual technology, eDVD discs are compatible with all DVD players.

In addition to these general categories of DVD projects, you may find clients that are involved in non-DVD activities which use some of the same production technologies. Specifically, an investment in a video encoding system such as that included in Sonic DVD Creator may enable your facility to serve clients involved in broadcast, video-on-demand and other applications of MPEG encoding.

## What audio formats are typically used on the type of DVDs your clients will be releasing?

As we have seen above, the DVD-Video and DVD-Audio specifications support a wide variety of audio formats, including PCM (at a wide range of sample rates and word lengths), Dolby Digital and MPEG. A flexible palette of channel configurations (mono through multichannel surround) is also supported, as are optional additional formats such as DTS. This potentially adds up to a very complex audio production situation, particularly for DVD-Video, where up to eight parallel audio streams may be used in a single title set.

In actual practice, the type of audio used will vary depending on the type of title. A facility designed to produce feature-length DVDs will likely need to be able to provide surround-sound encoding in Dolby Digital and MPEG formats, depending on the release region. For DVD-Audio titles, high-resolution multichannel pre-mastering capabilities will be expected, while for music video and karaoke DVD-Videos, CD-quality stereo PCM audio may be sufficient.

## What is your expected volume of work?

Depending on your assessment of the needs of your market, you may be planning to develop your DVD facility gradually, or to jump right into full-scale production. Your anticipated volume of work will determine your need for throughput, which greatly influences the architecture of your production system.

High volume production – more than 20 to 30 titles per year – generally demands a workflow that is collaborative and parallel rather than separate and sequential. Workgroup throughput may be maximized with the incorporation of batch encoding capabilities, allowing more efficient allocation of facility resources.

In a workgroup environment, the number of discrete workstations you design into your system will determine the specific capabilities you assign to each station. However, even if your current volume or budget dictate a single-station solution, an integrated environment of modular, upgradable components allows you to tailor a system to your current needs without limiting your ability to grow as business expands.

## What are your company's existing areas of expertise, and in what areas do additional skills need to be developed?

DVD production is not really a single discipline, but rather a process that integrates existing fields such as video post-production, audio engineering, graphic design and multimedia authoring. As with any service business, your clients will come to you not simply for the equipment you own but for the skill with which you use it.

If your business is already involved in media production, you can bring to DVD the expertise particular to your areas of specialization. Because the format is new, however, and its requirements so broad, you may well find areas where the collective knowledge base of your staff needs strengthening to operate your DVD facility effectively. Options include hiring additional staff with the required skills, or re-purposing existing staff via training courses and hands-on experience with the production system.

The pace at which a given facility extends its expertise into new areas depends, once again, on who its clients are and what services they need. If history is any guide, however, there is no time like the present to begin developing skills for the next generation of technology. In home video, for instance, the volume of production skyrocketed after DVD's consumer appeal was confirmed by a strong launch. Post production houses that took DVD seriously early on have naturally been well positioned to capitalize on the current boom, while others have been struggling to catch up. Similarly, mastering houses that embraced CD-Audio thrived during the re-issue boom that followed the format's popularization, while those that saw mastering only in terms of phonograph records, did not survive the transition.

Listed below are the functions that will need to be covered by a DVD production facility staff. In a large facility, each function may be a separate position. In a smaller operation, individual operators may need to cover

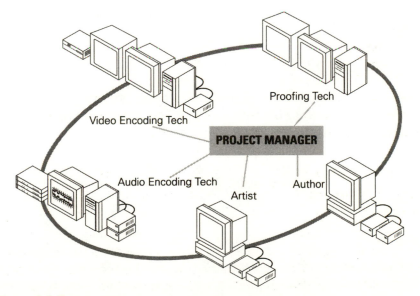

**Figure 9.5** Typical division of labour in a DVD production workgroup.

multiple tasks. In a multi-station workgroup configuration, one individual may be able to set up and start a process at one station (video encoding, for instance) and then move to a different station to continue work on a different aspect of production.

## Producer

The producer may be the client, a third party hired by the client, or someone on-staff at the DVD facility. Whatever the case, the producer is ultimately responsible for the end-product of the DVD production process. Responsibilities include defining the content, functionality and feel of the title in the project planning phase, as well as overseeing production, hiring talent, and choosing other members of the production team. A strong overall understanding of the capabilities and limitations of DVD, as well as the production process, is more important than hands-on skills in any particular area.

## Project manager

The project manager is responsible for scheduling workflow and milestones, the timely execution of production and the completion of projects within budget. A thorough understanding is required of each step in the DVD preparation process, as well as the relationship between steps. An efficient project manager should be able efficiently to manage multiple complex productions, including working with clients to define expectations, tracking the progress of diverse production elements, and coordinating parallel processes.

## Graphic designer

By defining the 'look and feel' of the graphic design, the artist sets the tone for the user's experience of the title. Graphics play a role not only as content but also in navigation. The artist thus needs both expertise in computer-based graphic production techniques and a thorough understanding of user-interface design. In addition, knowledge of design issues specific to both NTSC and PAL television is helpful, including awareness of aspect ratios, safe areas and colour ranges.

## Author

The author integrates all content elements and builds a title's navigational structure. Responsibilities include defining menu 'hot spots' and programing button links, as well as proofing to ensure compliance with the approved title design. Effective authoring depends not only on familiarity with media integration and interactive navigation design, but also on a thorough knowledge of common file formats for media assets. The advanced author will also be able to program register usage for score-keeping or conditional branching, and to integrate DVD-Video or DVD-Audio content with Web applications and other materials stored in the DVD-Others zone.

## Video encoding technician

The video encoder can have a substantial impact on the quality of video encoding, particularly if the source material requires pre-processing, filtering or manual editing. The ideal background for this position is previous experience with digital video compression systems or in video production. For feature film releases, it may take 3 to 6 months of hands-on work with the encoding system to develop advanced skills in manipulating MPEG compression variables, which are needed for optimal results. For corporate applications, experience with Avid or Media 100 NLV editing systems will typically provide the required expertise.

## Audio pre-mastering engineer

Mastering engineers with extensive experience in preparing material for CD-Audio release have the required foundation of critical listening and sound enhancement skills for DVD-Audio, including level matching, EQ, dynamics processing, and editing. However, the range of options in DVD-Audio titles make them potentially far more complex than CDs, and it may take pre-mastering engineers a while to adapt their techniques to the new possibilities.

## Audio encoding technician

Basic understanding of audio formats, interfacing and production is required, but the crucial attributes for an audio encoder are a good ear and a sense – which may have to be developed on the job – of how surround-sound formats should sound when properly encoded. Ideally, the audio encoder will also know how to adjust Dolby Digital encoding parameters.

# Chapter 10

# Production system scenarios

Having thought through the issues raised in the questions in the previous chapter, you are now ready to get down to specifying your title preparation environment. Scenarios for organizing DVD production fall into three basic categories: the networked DVD workgroup (minimum of two workstations), packages designed for integration with non-linear video editing systems, and general purpose standalone publishing solutions. These categories need not be hard and fast, however, because a well-conceived family of DVD production products will make it possible to start out with a core system tailored to current requirements, and to upgrade later, as needs grow.

In general, a networked workgroup is designed to support high-throughput production operations, such as facilities targeted towards feature film titles for the home video market. These facilities will be optimized specifically for DVD, supporting the production of multiple titles simultaneously. An exploration of the considerations involved in setting up such an environment is found in this chapter.

The other two categories of production environments cover situations which call for DVD publishing on a smaller scale, where creating DVDs may not be the primary business activity. Packages that integrate with NLE systems, for instance, are specifically designed to support DVD publishing in environments where video post-production is the main focus.

Standalone solutions, on the other hand, are intended to support a very diverse range of DVD publishing activities. The longer DVD has been on the market, the more people are finding different ways of using it. Thus the demand for small-scale DVD publishing capabilities may be found not only in professional settings such as corporate AV departments and museums, but also in the homes of video enthusiasts and 'pro-sumer' videographers.

Note that because still-image editing is normally handled in a graphics application (e.g. Adobe® Photoshop®) which is easily added to any computer-hosted DVD production system, considerations related to graphic arts production are not covered in the following discussion.

# Integrated NLE/DVD publishing

Over the last decade, digital production techniques have transformed all areas of media production, bringing workstation-based tools to the fore. In settings such as post-production houses, in-house corporate video departments and advertising agencies, video facilities are now commonly designed around non-linear editing workstations from manufacturers such as Avid and Media 100.

The quality and capabilities of NLE systems have increased dramatically over the years. Unfortunately, the medium often used for distribution of their output – VHS – is not technically capable of capturing this improved quality, and lacks a convenient way to navigate to a specific point in the overall program. DVD, on the other hand, offers excellent video (and audio) quality, the convenience of random access, and the ability to play back in both DVD set-top devices and personal computers.

To serve this market, DVD tools may be designed to integrate directly with NLE systems, creating a natural flow from the editing process through creation of a finished DVD. Sonic DVD Fusion, for instance, allows edited video files from Avid, Media 100 and QuickTime-based NLE systems to be transcoded in the digital domain directly into high-quality MPEG-2 video, eliminating the need to first lay video content off to tape. This ensures the highest video quality and avoids the signal degradation that can occur with digital-to-analog and analog-to-digital conversion. DVD Fusion also supports audio transcoding direct to Dolby Digital 5.1. After building menus, defining navigation and proofing, the finished content may be written to DVD-R or DVD-RAM for distribution.

The integration of DVD publishing with NLE systems means that post houses, advertising agencies and independent producers may add DVD capabilities efficiently, without reorganizing their overall workflow into a DVD-centric model. It also allows video facilities to generate added revenue by offering direct-to-DVD publishing services to their clients.

Ideally, a DVD package designed for integration with an NLE system should include the following key features:

- direct transcoding of video and audio files;
- fully DVD-compliant MPEG-2 video VBR and CBR encoding;
- WYSIWYG, drag-and-drop authoring;
- direct recording to DVD-R;
- integrated DVD-Video and DVD-ROM production;
- Dolby-certified Dolby Digital 5.1 encoding;
- eDVD™ support for Web-connected hybrid titles;
- a user interface that is intuitive for video professionals.

# Standalone DVD publishing

Standalone DVD publishing solutions are designed for low-volume settings where DVD is not a primary focus, or where limited space, staffing or capital budget are more important factors than high throughput. For example, in-house corporate communications departments or multimedia developers that are still primarily focused on linear video or CD-ROM may find that a single, trained operator working on one machine may be enough to meet initial DVD needs. Event videographers, meanwhile, may use DVD to deliver recordings of weddings, anniversaries and birthday parties to their customers. Even home enthusiasts who own a video camcorder may want to create their own Hollywood-like DVD-Video content. We will focus here on professional applications.

**Figure 10.1** An all-in-one system for DVD title production might include external video monitoring and audio gear.

Like a DVD workgroup, an all-in-one system must be able to handle all the title preparation and authoring steps covered in earlier chapters. However, in a single-user setting, the steps will be handled sequentially rather than in parallel. So the authoring package needs to be not only flexible, but also fast in terms of both ease-of-use and processing power.

Ease-of-use is crucial because the smaller the production staff, the more likely that a given person will handle more than one facet of production. If a video encoder, for instance, is so complex that only a highly-specialized operator can obtain good results, it is not of much use in a jack-of-all-trades production setting. A well-designed single-user system will offer the same high-quality end-results as a professional workgroup, without presenting the user with an overly complex interface.

Overall interface design should recognize that the user may not be authoring DVD on a daily basis; to keep the process on track, applications should actively assist the operator. Sonic DVDit!, for instance, uses features such as templates and drag-and-drop file conversion to keep the authoring process as straightforward as possible.

**Figure 10.2** The interface of Sonic DVDit! is designed with an emphasis on ease-of-use.

In an all-in-one setting, a system that is slow to perform file conversion or data multiplexing can result in an operator who wastes a lot of time waiting around. Productivity can be maximized by choosing a system powerful enough to handle processor-intensive operations quickly, and which allows unsupervised encoding and multiplexing to be scheduled during off-peak times or overnight. Professional users who foresee growth in their DVD activities will also want to consider whether their DVD package is reconfigurable for use in a workgroup production setting when demand grows.

The standalone publishing system category covers a diversity of situations, but if such a system will be used for professional or pro-sumer applications, it should generally include the following features:

- DVD-compliant transcoding of AVI or QuickTime files to MPEG-2;
- WYSIWYG, drag-and-drop authoring;
- Direct recording to DVD-R;
- integrated DVD-Video and DVD-ROM production;
- intuitive, easy-to-use interface.

# The DVD production workgroup

Networked workgroups are the preferred system configuration for any setting in which throughput is a top priority. To produce titles efficiently, production must be carried out in parallel, drawing from a common asset base and with information passed back and forth between system components. By distributing production tasks amongst several workstations, work on different aspects of a title can move forward at the same time, and multiple titles can be in production at once.

In a workgroup environment, audio editing can take place while an author is laying out a title, or video encoding for a new project can begin while proofing takes place on the previous project. Each step may be handled by a specialist, but without the traditional obstacles to interaction and revision. With efficient scheduling of equipment and personnel resources, a workgroup-based facility delivers high volume, fast turnaround, and – most importantly – higher-quality titles.

In order to maximize productivity, a workgroup for DVD production should have the following characteristics:

- shared resources – hard drives, I/O devices, etc.;
- iterative, non-linear work flow;

- be modular and expandable;
- capable of Bit Budget™ planning;
- multitrack High-Density Audio editing, mixing;
- multitask/multiproject capability;
- networked by high-speed LAN;
- no bottlenecks;
- full proofing at every station;
- seamless playback of files on network with guaranteed bandwidth;
- data transfer station for archiving, formatting, and disc image creation;
- automation capabilities for asset encoding and title formatting/final output;
- eDVD™ support for Web-connected hybrid titles.

## Workgroup configurations

Depending on the volume and type of titles to be produced, DVD workgroups may be configured in a variety of ways. Facilities oriented towards preparing feature films for the home video market, for instance, will generally be set up with a minimum of four workstations: audio, video, authoring and

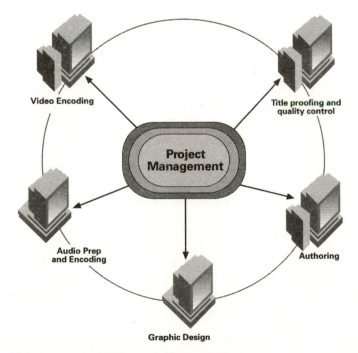

**Figure 10.3** A networked DVD production workgroup.

proofing. A fifth station for graphics and subtitling will increase the overall throughput. In higher-volume facilities, additional workstations may be added as needed for still greater throughput in any or all of these areas.

In a typical workgroup, the video station is equipped for VBR video encoding, and simultaneous real-time capture of video and stereo audio. The audio station is equipped for capture and compression of surround audio in Dolby Digital and perhaps also MPEG formats, and may also run a DVD-capable audio pre-mastering package (e.g. SonicStudio HD). The authoring station would run the authoring component of the DVD production package, and would include video and audio decoding for proofing. The proofing station would naturally be equipped with decoding hardware for proofing as well.

In some settings, such as facilities intended primarily to produce DVD-Video karaoke titles, surround-sound capabilities may not be required, and a three-station workgroup may be sufficient. In this case, audio and video capture/compression might also be combined into one station. In even lower volume settings, authoring and proofing might also be combined into one station. Flexible design of the production system will allow for such compact configurations without compromising the possibility of later expansion.

Because a workgroup allows files from one station to be accessed from elsewhere on the network, the use of server-based automated processes is a logical extension of the workgroup concept. In Sonic DVD Creator, for instance, source assets may be batch encoded with AutoSonic™, while HyperMux™ can analyse, multiplex and store a title's logical image on a separate, network-connected format server. Automating and scheduling tasks that do not normally require constant oversight frees qualified personnel to concentrate on the creative and quality assurance aspects of title production.

## Network and storage considerations

Perhaps the biggest difference between a workgroup and an all-in-one configuration is the workgroup's use of a Local Area Network (LAN). The network allows the individual workstations efficient access to component media files residing on other workstations. It also enables intelligent integration of the production process (i.e. the authoring tool can reference a video stream on the video workstation).

Ideally, the network will offer dedicated channels with uninterrupted bandwidth to access remote files and play them back in real time without dropouts. A Fibre-Channel Storage Area Network (SAN) offers an ideal high-performance environment where centrally located storage may be accessed at 100 Megabytes per second speeds from multiple workstations.

A DVD workgroup with multiple projects in production simultaneously will require substantial hard drive storage space, at least 2.2 times the size of the finished disc image, for each title. For each DVD-5, for instance, that works out to about 11 GB.

In a Fibre-Channel-based workgroup, a 36 GB RAID (redundant hard-disk array) should provide sufficient storage to accommodate multiple projects simultaneously. In typical video production settings, a minimum of 9 GB of storage is recommended for audio capture, 23 GB for video, and 23 GB for authoring. As with any data storage system, a consistent backup regimen is highly recommended.

## *Peripheral equipment*

Workgroups and all-in-one systems share the need for peripheral equipment to complete the production environment. For instance, a video monitor is required at the audio/video capture and compression station(s) for viewing video. An audio monitoring system is also needed; the minimum audio system would be a pair of speakers driven by a power amplifier. For surround-sound titles, a 5.1 channel surround playback system will be needed (left front, centre, right front, left surround, right surround and subwoofer).

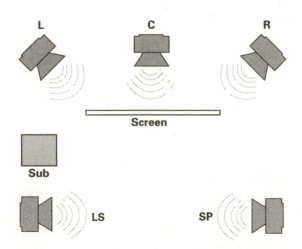

**Figure 10.4** A surround sound monitoring environment.

In order to capture video and audio from tape (rather than converting files from a non-linear video editor or digital audio workstation), playback decks for the source video and audio formats will be required. The specific formats needed will depend on the formats typically used by the suppliers of source material to the facility. D1 and Digital BetaCam are the most likely formats for home video; in corporate work, Betacam SP and DV are also popular. Depending on the video encoding tool, other formats may require special interfacing hardware. A black-burst-to-word-sync converter may also be required in some set-ups.

**Figure 10.5** The Tascam DA-88 8-track audio recorder is commonly used for multichannel mixes.

If most of a facility's titles will use stereo audio only, the audio may be provided on the audio tracks of the videotape, meaning that a separate audio machine may not be needed. Surround mixes, however, will generally be supplied separately on a digital multitrack format, such as the Tascam DA-88, which can accommodate 5.1 discrete channels of sound. Alternatively, stereo or surround tracks may come to the facility in digital form from an audio workstation.

## Working environment

Once the configuration of a facility's DVD production system and peripheral equipment is decided, it is possible to begin thinking about the working environment for title preparation. Considerations include efficient physical layout of work areas and machine rooms, providing sufficient electrical service, designing light sources for minimal monitor glare, and providing adequate ventilation and temperature control for the amount of people and equipment in a given workspace.

The best layout for a DVD workgroup will depend largely on the working style of the production team. A workgroup's network may allow workstations to be physically separated in different rooms or even buildings, but easy physical access from one operator to another may be preferred where a cohesive team approach to title development is a priority.

Naturally, adequate physical space must be allowed for each station in the workgroup, as well as for the peripheral gear relating to each station's function. In the case of a video capture station, this may mean allowing for the video monitor to be positioned next to the computer monitor to minimize strain in looking back and forth.

The deck for playing source video tapes may be located in a separate machine room and controlled remotely. In workgroups automated with AutoSonic, e-mails and pages may be automatically sent to machine room operators when tape changes or other system needs arise. If multiple video capture stations will be using the same video deck, a 9-pin switcher may be used for switching control over the deck between the various stations. Alternatively, some operators may find it more convenient to have the machine close at hand for easy tape loading, and to retain hands-on control of jog/shuttle transport functions.

**Figure 10.6** A DVD-Video production suite.

The main consideration for audio stations is to provide an acoustical environment in which it is possible to hear program material accurately for critical listening. It is also important to be able to monitor at different levels without disturbing or distracting others, and to be able to listen closely without hearing noise from other areas. For facilities with surround-sound encoding capability, a surround playback system must be properly set up (based on ITU standards) to allow QC of the encoded audio signal.

# Conclusion

DVD is a state-of-the-art medium for the delivery of high-impact interactive multimedia. Home video, music, interactive entertainment, learning, and corporate presentations are all areas that can benefit from this family of formats. Given this broad range of potential users and applications, DVD production offers a unique opportunity for production facilities to build on their existing strengths while expanding their business into new areas.

As we have seen, a comprehensive DVD production solution brings together trained operators with a set of specialized hardware and software, a network, and an appropriate physical workspace. Just as DVD itself offers integrated, interactive media presentation, a DVD production facility works best when it is an integrated environment, facilitating interaction amongst its component parts. Additionally, just as DVD is a flexible format, a DVD production system need not be a generic, one-size-fits-all formula. In a swiftly evolving technical and business climate, the wisest investment is a platform that is not only tailored to today's needs, but is also easily expandable as those needs grow and change.

Together with creativity, a clear vision, and a thorough understanding of the considerations outlined in this book, the right production environment lays the foundation for success in the rapidly expanding world of DVD.

# Glossary

**16:9** – widescreen aspect ratio (1.78:1) used in DVD and DTV; a close compromise to the 1.85:1 aspect ratio used in film.

**4:3** – the aspect ratio (also expressed as 1.33:1) of a standard television screen.

**AC-3** – see Dolby Digital.

**activate** – to execute the command associated with a button.

**Album** – the program on one side of a DVD-Audio disc; each album may contain up to nine Groups.

**AMG** – Audio Manager; see AMG/AOTT and AMG/AVTT.

**AMG/AOTT (Audio Manager/Audio-only Title)** – the content directory on a DVD-Audio disc that is used by smart Audio-only players.

**AMG/AVTT (Audio Manager/Audio and Video Title)** – the content directory on a DVD-Audio disc that is used by players that have video output (Audio-with-Video players and Universal players).

**AMGM** – Audio Manager Menu, the main visual menu for an AMG/AVTT DVD-Audio volume; the destination of the TITLE button on a DVD-Audio player remote.

**anamorphic** – a widescreen (16:9) image horizontally squeezed to fit into a 4:3 frame. When played back on a standard (4:3) TV, the image may be viewed in its anamorphic state, letterboxed, or pan/scan.

**AOB** – see Audio Object.

**AOBS** – see Audio Object Set.

**API** – applications programing interface.

**aspect ratio** – the relationship between the horizontal dimension and the vertical dimension of an image.

**asset list** – a complete list of the various audio, video, graphic, text, and subpicture elements included in a DVD title; prepared as part of the production planning process.

**assets** – the various audio, video, graphic, text, and subpicture elements included in a DVD title.

**Audio Object (AOB)** – the basic unit of DVD-Audio presentation data; made up of one or more Tracks (songs or compositions) of audio, optionally accompanied by still images and/or Real Time Text.

**Audio Object Set (AOBS)** – the collection of AOBs that make up the presentation data referenced by an audio title.

**Audio Still Video (ASV)** – the basic unit of graphics in DVD-Audio. An ASV is composed of an MPEG still, plus optional subpicture unit overlay (SPU), and highlight information (HLI).

**Audio Still Video Unit (ASVU)** – in DVD-Audio, a collection of up to 99 ASVs that is available for display over an ASVU range, which extends over one or more audio tracks. The total of all the images in an ASVU may not exceed 2 MB.

**Audio Text Data** – in DVD-Audio, text that is intended for the display of static information that is not synchronized to the audio program, including Album title, Group name, and Track title.

**Audio Title (ATT)** – the domain encompassing the logical structure of the main (non-menu) content on a DVD-Audio disc.

**Audio-with-Video player** – a DVD-Audio player that has video outputs; uses the AMG/AVTT content directory on DVD-Audio discs.

**Audio_TS** – the file directory on a DVD where DVD-Audio data is stored.

**authoring** – a media integration process in which a set of individual media elements (audio, video, graphics and text) are combined into a unified whole, and navigation between the various parts is defined.

**auto-activate** – a button state in which the command associated with the button is activated as soon as the button is selected, without the viewer having to press ENTER.

**autoplay** – an authoring parameter that commands the disc to begin playing a given program as soon as the disc is loaded into the player.

**B-pictures** – bi-directional pictures in MPEG-2; reconstructed by referring to information in both a previous and a subsequent frame.

**background image** – motion video or 24-bit colour still image that is used as the backdrop on menu screens.

**bandwidth** – the rate at which a given playback or transmission system is able to pass data (see data transfer rate); usually expressed in bits or bytes per second.

**bit** – the smallest unit of information in a digital file or stream.

**Bit Budget™** – the allocation of a DVD's overall data capacity and data bandwidth to the various audio, video, graphic, text, and subpicture elements included in the asset list.

**bonding** – the process of laminating together two 0.6-mm substrates to form a finished DVD.

**Browseable** – in DVD-Audio, a display mode for still images in which each image has a defined minimum and maximum on-screen duration, but the user is allowed to skip forward using the remote control.

**browser** – software that allows a computer to view HTML pages on the World Wide Web.

**button highlight** – the rectangular region of a menu screen that is reserved for each menu choice.

**byte** – a unit of data made up of 8 bits.

**CBR** – see Constant Bit-rate.

**CD** – see Compact Disc.

**CD-ROM (Compact Disc-Read Only Memory)** – a collection of formats used for storing and retrieving data on a CD, typically in a computer-hosted context.

**cDVD** – a variation of DVD developed by Sonic Solutions that allows a DVD-Video program to be written to CD-ROM and played back from a computer hosted CD-ROM drive using special player software.

**Cell** – a section of a VOB; the smallest unit of presentation data that may be addressed directly when navigating during branching or other interactivity.

**chapter** – a navigational marker allowing a PGC to go to a specific Cell in a VOB; typically used to allow direct access to individual scenes.

**codec** – the generic term for compression/decompression algorithms that are used to reduce the storage and transmission requirements of video, audio and graphics files.

**colour-depth** – in computer graphics, the total number of possible colours supported for display in a given image format or with a given computer and monitor. Usually given as the number of bits available to express the saturation value of each of the three component colours (red, green, blue) for each pixel (i.e. 8-bit, 24-bit, etc.).

**Compact Disc** – an optical medium for storage and playback of digital audio and data.

**component video** – a video system (analog or digital) in which the picture information is maintained as three components, such as RGB (red, green, blue).

**composite video** – a video system in which all the picture information (including sync pulse) is mixed into a single signal.

**conforming** – in video post-production, editing audio tracks to be in sync with a video master.

**Constant Bit-rate (CBR)** – a video encoding method in which bits are allocated evenly across the entire length of the program.

**Content Scrambling System (CSS)** – see encryption.

**copy protection** – technologies used to prevent the copying of analog signals or digital output streams from a DVD-Video or DVD-Audio disc.

**CSS** – see encryption.

**data transfer rate** – the rate at which digital data are retrieved from a storage medium or transmitted through a transmission medium. Usually expressed as either bits or bytes per second.

**decoder** – the hardware or software used to recreate a video or audio signal from an encoded stream.

**Direct Stream Digital (DSD)** – a digital audio encoding method in which the waveform is measured at a sampling rate of 2.8 MHz (2.8 million times per second), and changes in direction of the amplitude (rising or falling) are stored.

**DirectShow** – an API supporting MPEG-2 playback on computers running the Microsoft Windows operating system.

**disc image** – a complete set of files containing the logical and presentation data of a DVD volume, formatted in DVD's UDF file system and ready to be output to a DVD master or DVD-R one-off.

**DLT (Digital Linear Tape)** – the master format normally used for DVD when the title will be replicated at a plant.

**Dolby Digital (AC-3)** – an audio codec developed by Dolby Laboratories using perceptual coding to deliver audio in low bandwidth settings. Playback support for Dolby Digital is mandated for all DVD players. In DVD, Dolby Digital bit-rates range from 192 kbps for mono/stereo program to 384–448 kbps for 5.1 channel surround sound.

**double-sided** – a disc, such as a DVD-10 or DVD-18, that has information moulded into both of its laminated polycarbonate substrates.

**downmix** – the combining of a multichannel audio mix into a stereo program.

**DSD** – see Direct Stream Digital.

**DTS** – an audio codec developed by Digital Theater Systems for delivering 5.1 channel surround sound in theatres and consumer electronics devices.

**DTV** – the digital television standard for the US, defined by the Advanced Television Systems Committee.

**dual-layer** – a method of constructing DVDs (DVD-9 and DVD-18) that allows a single disc image to extend over two data surfaces read from the same side of a disc, thereby nearly doubling the capacity of the side.

**dummy PGC** – a Program Chain that does not include a list of cells to play from a VOB. Used to group multiple commands together by using only the pre- and post-command areas. Dummy PGCs may also be used to move between Video Title Sets.

**DVD Forum** – A consortium of more than 100 member companies, including consumer electronics manufacturers, computer companies and content owners, which is responsible for defining and maintaining the DVD specification.

**DVD navigator** – a software module that allows DVD-Video titles to play back on computers.

**DVD-5** – a DVD disc with a capacity of 4.7 GB; single-sided, single layer.

**DVD-9** – a DVD disc with a capacity of 8.54 GB; single-sided, with dual layers.

**DVD-10** – a DVD disc with a capacity of 9.4 GB; double-sided, with a single layer on each side.

**DVD-14** – a DVD disc that is dual layer on one side and single layer on the other. DVD-14 is not part of the official DVD specification.

**DVD-18** – a two-sided DVD disc with a capacity of 17.08 GB; dual layer on both sides.

**DVD-Audio** – a high-fidelity audio-centric format provided for in Book C of the DVD specification.

**DVD-Audio player** – a playback device for DVD-Audio discs; variations include simple Audio-only player, smart Audio-only player, and Universal player.

**DVD-Audio zone** – a directory (AUDIO_TS) on a DVD disc containing all of the data elements for playing back the disc's DVD-Audio content.

**DVD-Others zone** – that portion of the file structure on a DVD disc that is not within the VIDEO_TS or AUDIO_TS directories.

**DVD-Random Access Memory (DVD-RAM)** – a rewriteable DVD format defined by Book E of the DVD specification.

**DVD-Recordable (DVD-R)** – a recordable, write-once DVD format defined by Book D of the DVD specification.

**DVD-Rewritable (DVD-RW)** – a rewriteable DVD format defined by Book F of the DVD specification.

**DVD-ROM** – a general-purpose data format provided for in Book A of the DVD specification. DVD-Video and DVD-Audio are specific applications that extend the basic DVD-ROM specification.

**DVD-ROM drive** – a computer-hosted reader for playback of DVD-ROM discs. With additional hardware and/or software, a computer with a DVD-ROM drive may also play DVD-Video and DVD-Audio content.

**DVD-Video** – a high-quality video-centric format provided for in Book B of the DVD specification.

**DVD-Video player** – a player that hooks to a television set and plays back DVD-Video specification discs.

**DVD-Video zone** – a directory (VIDEO_TS) on a DVD disc containing all of the data elements for playback of the disc's DVD-Video content.

**eDVD** – a DVD-Video disc authored with Sonic Solutions technology that enables Web-connectivity. When an eDVD is played in a computer-hosted DVD-ROM drive, links embedded in the DVD-Video content enable navigation of content displayed in a browser.

**elemental assets** – the video, audio, graphics and subpicture files that are combined into VOBs during production of a DVD title.

**encoder** – the hardware or software used to convert a video or audio signal or file into a specific format; often involves use of an algorithm for reducing the amount of data.

**encryption** – a copy protection measure used in DVD in which data are scrambled to prevent DVD players from recreating a valid signal from an unauthorized copy of a DVD disc.

**EQ (equalization)** – changing the frequency content of an audio program through the use of filters that boost or cut in specific frequency ranges.

**featurette** – a short program included on a feature-film DVD as added-value content, generally explaining the making of the main feature or giving background related to the events depicted.

**field** – in interlaced video, one of two alternating sets of scan lines that combine to make a complete video frame. In DVD, video may be stored either as field-based video or as frame-based video. On playback, both types of video are output as field-based (interlaced) video for viewing on standard television monitors.

**formatting** – the creation of a set of files which complies with the DVD-Video or DVD-Audio format specification. Involves multiplexing presentation data (audio, video, subpictures) and incorporating the PGCs into the information areas of each volume's managers.

**frame** – in video and film, a single complete picture; two fields of interlaced video.

**General parameters (GPRMs)** – memory locations used by the currently playing DVD program for basic computation or for storing values. Sixteen 16-bit memory locations are available. Examples of typical GPRM usage include remembering which segments of an interactive story have already been viewed, or keeping track of the number of lives a character has left in a game.

**Gigabyte (GB)** – used in relation to DVD, a Gigabyte equals one billion bytes, rather than the $1024^3$ bytes definition used in the computing industry.

**GOP (Group of Pictures)** – in MPEG video, a sequence of pictures (frames) defined by a pattern of I-pictures, B-pictures and P-pictures.

**GPRMs** – see General parameters

**Group** – in DVD-Audio, a play list specifying the playback order of a number of audio Titles; a given Track may be referenced by more than one Group. There may be no more than 99 Tracks total within a single Group.

**hDVD** – an extension of the DVD-Video format, developed by Sonic Solutions, which allows the creation of DVD-Video titles using High Definition video. hDVDs may be played back from a computer-hosted DVD-ROM drive using special player software.

**highlight** – see button highlight.

**hot spot** – see button highlight.

**HTML** – Hypertext Markup Language, the format used by Web browsers to display Web pages.

**hybrid title** – a DVD with content stored outside the DVD-Video or DVD-Audio zones, which may be accessed by users with DVD-ROM drives.

**I-pictures** – in MPEG-2, pictures that are encoded using intra-frame compression only, and contain all the information needed to reconstruct an individual frame of video.

**Index** – a reference point to a portion of an audio track (Cell); there may be up to 99 Indices within a single track.

**inter-frame compression** – in MPEG video compression, a data-reduction technique in which only the information necessary to describe the differences between a series of adjacent video frames is retained. When the encoded material is played back, a decoder extrapolates from the stored information to re-create a complete set of discrete frames.

**interlaced** – video in which a complete frame is scanned in two passes (fields) of alternate lines (odd lines, even lines).

**intra-frame compression** – in MPEG video compression, a data-reduction technique in which the colour information within individual video frames is re-coded to express redundant information more efficiently. Depending on the degree of compression, adjacent colours that are similar to one another may be encoded as if they are the same colour.

**inverse telecine** – the removal of redundant fields introduced into NTSC video during the film-to-video (telecine) transfer process.

**letterbox** – a widescreen image shown in full on a 1.33:1 screen, with black borders along the top and bottom.

**Linear PCM** – see Pulse Code Modulation.

**logical format** – the structure used to organize the storage of data on a storage medium; the logical format of DVD is UDF.

**Manager** – the first directory that a DVD player reads to determine what content is present on a given disc.

**menu** – in DVD, a screen or succession of screens offering the viewer options for playback navigation or setup.

**menu background** – motion video or 24-bit colour still image that is used as the backdrop on menu screens.

**Meridian Lossless Packing (MLP)** – a lossless data reduction technique which allows PCM audio to be stored more efficiently without any loss of fidelity; mandated player support for MLP playback is part of the DVD-Audio specification.

**metalizing** – the application of the reflective coatings that allow the pits moulded into the surface of a DVD to be read by an optical pickup.

**micro-UDF** – a subset of the UDF file system (see Universal Disc Format) that includes additional constraints to facilitate use in an inexpensive playback device, such as a set-top player.

**mixed density disc** – a dual-layer DVD combining a conventional (CD-density) layer with a high-density DVD layer.

**motion menu** – a menu with a motion video background.

**MLP** – see Meridian Lossless Packing.

**MPEG** – Motion Picture Experts Group, an organization that defines encoding techniques for video and audio programs.

**MPEG Audio** – audio encoding algorithms defined by MPEG for low bit-rate storage and transmission of stereo and multichannel (up to 7.1) program; may utilize variable bit-rate audio encoding.

**MPEG-1** – a video compression scheme developed by MPEG and used in Video CD (White Book). Playback support is mandated for DVD players, but MPEG-2 is generally used on DVD discs.

**MPEG-2** – a video compression scheme developed by MPEG and mandated in DVD players. MPEG-2 uses both intra-frame and inter-frame compression to store video more efficiently (reduce data redundancy) and, where necessary, to discard information (based on perceptual coding techniques) that is likely to have the least impact on image quality.

**multi-angle** – a DVD-Video feature allowing a single video stream to incorporate up to nine parallel video programs (which may or may not be different angles of the same scene).

**multichannel** – audio intended for playback over three or more speakers; see surround sound.

**multiplex (MUX)** – the interleaving of data from multiple elemental streams (i.e. video, audio, subpictures) into a single stream.

**NLE** – non-linear editing; computer-based video editing systems in which the data to be edited are stored on a random access medium (such as a hard-disk) rather than on a linear medium such as videotape.

**NTSC** – National Television Systems Committee, the organization which developed the standards used for analog television transmission in the US (also adopted in Japan, Canada and Korea). NTSC television uses 525 lines (480 of which are used for picture information) at frame rates of 30 fps (60 fields) for black-and-white and 29.97 fps for colour.

**P-pictures** – predictive pictures in MPEG-2; reconstructed based on the nearest previous I- or P-picture.

**PAL** – the Phase Alternate Line television standard used in Europe and various other regions throughout the world. PAL video normally uses 625 scan lines (576 lines of vertical picture information) at a frame rate of 25 fps (50 fields).

**palette** – in DVD, the set of 16 colours that is available for use in subpicture overlays in the current Program Chain.

**pan/scan** – a method of displaying widescreen content on a standard video monitor. A 4:3 viewing area is moved around over the original widescreen image to follow the most important action in the frame, while material on either side of this area is left out.

**parental control** – a system allowing the owner of a DVD-Video player to set the player to block playback of material beyond a given rating level.

**PCM** – see Pulse Code Modulation.

**perceptual coding** – an overall approach to data reduction algorithms for video and audio in which decisions about which data to discard are based on assumptions about human perception.

**PGC** – see Program Chain.

**pit-density** – the number of pits that can be moulded into the surface of an optical disc. DVD uses shorter pit lengths and tighter tracks to achieve a pit-density more than four times greater than CD.

**pits** – a series of tiny impressions moulded in a spiral track into the surface of a CD or a DVD. Binary code is represented by varying the length of the pits. Once the disc is coated with a reflective layer, the optical pickup of a playback device can read the difference in reflectivity between the pits and the surrounding land area.

**pixel** – a unit of measurement in computer graphics (the smallest individually addressable unit of area on the screen); an individual dot in a computer graphic image.

**post-command** – a command at the end of a Program Chain, commonly used for tasks such as linking directly to another PGC, or returning to a main menu.

**pre-command** – a command at the start of a Program Chain; sets a playback condition for the VOBs that follow, such as which audio stream will be played.

**pre-processing** – the use of a digital noise reducer or low-pass filter to reduce high-energy noise in the video signal prior to encoding.

**Program Chain (PGC)** – the basic logical unit of the DVD specification; a set of instructions determining the conditions, timing and order of the playback of VOBs and (in DVD-Audio only) AOBs. In DVD-Video, a PGC may include a pre-command, a list of cells to be played from the referenced VOB, and a post-command.

**progressive scan** – in video, the writing of each frame entirely in one pass (non-interlaced).

**proofing** – the previewing of a project during authoring to check that it plays back as intended.

**PTT** – Part of Title; see chapter point.

**Pulse Code Modulation (PCM)** – a digital audio encoding method in which the amplitude of a waveform is measured at regular intervals and converted into a binary code that is stored as a series of pulses. The resolution of a PCM system is a function of both the sample rate and the word-length (number of bits per sample).

**Pure Audio disc** – a DVD-Audio disc that includes only audio content (no graphics, text or video) and the SAMG content directory.

**QuickTime** – a software platform for synchronized playback of a variety of video, audio, still picture, animation and other file types on Mac OS and Windows computers.

**random** – in DVD-Audio, a display mode for still images in which the order is randomly determined by the player.

**Real Time Text** – in DVD-Audio, text that is stored on disc as part of the audio stream, and may be synchronized to audio playback; may be used for lyrics, libretto, and running liner notes.

**regional coding** – a hardware-coded identifier that indicates the region (out of six worldwide) in which a DVD player is to be sold. A DVD-Video title may be coded to allow playback only on machines from one or more regions.

**replication** – the mass production of optical discs using injection-moulding techniques.

**reverse spiral** – refers to the read direction of the second layer of a continuous-play dual-layer DVD. The first layer is read from the centre of the disc to the outside, at which point the read optics refocus onto the second layer and begin reading from the outside back in towards the middle.

**RGB** – the red-green-blue form of component video; commonly used for computer monitors.

**rollover** – to move a computer's cursor over an on-screen button.

**safe area** – the portion of a video picture that will definitely be displayed on an NTSC television screen; excludes the outermost 5–10 per cent of the image on all sides.

**safe colours** – the range of colours that can be displayed by NTSC television, which has a more limited saturation range than the RGB video used in computer graphics.

**SAMG** – Simple Audio Manager; a mandatory content directory on DVD-Audio discs. SAMG is a sequential list of up to 314 tracks for linear, track-based navigation (similar to CD) on simple Audio-only players.

**sample-rate** – in digital audio, the number of times per second that the source waveform has been sampled (see Pulse Code Modulation).

**SDDS** – Sony Dynamic Digital Sound, an audio codec for delivering 7.1 channel surround sound in theatres and consumer electronics devices.

**sDVD** – a method developed by Sonic Solutions allowing DVD-Video material to be output in a data-reduced form for transmission over broadband networks including the Internet.

**segment-based re-encoding** – the ability of an encoding system to re-encode a portion of a given video program without having to re-encode the entire program.

**select** – to navigate to a button with the remote (or mouse).

**sequential** – in DVD-Audio, a display mode for still images in which the order is predetermined by the producer.

**shuffle** – in DVD-Audio, a display mode for still images in which the order is randomly determined by the player, but no image is repeated until every image has been shown.

**simple Audio-only player** – a DVD-Audio player that has no video output and uses the SAMG content directory, which supports only linear, track-based navigation of DVD-Audio discs.

**slide show** – in DVD-Video, a sequence of still video images pre-programed to advance automatically.

**slideshow** – in DVD-Audio, a display mode for still images in which each image is displayed for a predetermined amount of time.

**smart Audio-only player** – a DVD-Audio player that has no video output, but uses a disc's AMG/AOTT content directory, supporting hierarchical navigation based on groups; may include an LCD display to show song titles and other text information such as lyrics.

**SMART Content** – System Managed Audio Resource Technique; a DVD-Audio feature allowing definition of the relative level, panning and phase to be applied to each channel of a multichannel mix if that mix is down-mixed to stereo. A SMART down-mix of a given program will only be played if a discrete 2-channel mix of that program has not been included on the disc.

**still show** – in DVD-Video, a sequence of still video images that may be advanced manually by the user.

**storage capacity** – the amount of data that can be stored on a given storage medium. The storage capacity of DVDs ranges from 4.7 GB to 17.08 GB.

**storyboard** – a set of rough visual mock-ups that are used to help define a program's contents and plan production.

**subpicture overlay** – images that are generated by the DVD player on playback and appear on top of background video or still images. Used for subtitles and for highlights on menu screens.

**substrate** – in DVD, the plastic parts that are moulded during replication; a finished DVD is constructed from two 0.6-mm substrates bonded together.

**Super Audio CD** – a disc format proposed by Sony and Philips that is based on the same physical and logical structure as DVD but stores audio in the DSD format.

**surround sound** – audio playback configurations in which some of the channels are intended to be played back from the side or rear of the listener rather than only from the front. Common surround configurations include Lt/Rt (left, centre, right, and surround channels) and 5.1 (left, centre, right, left surround, right surround and low-frequency effects channels).

**System parameters** – memory locations used by a DVD player to remember default settings such as language, aspect ratio, and Parental Rating level. System parameters may be set either by the viewer or by a DVD title as it plays.

**telecine** – the process of transferring film to video.

**Title** – in DVD-Audio, a set of Tracks. The order of Title playback is defined by Groups (playlists).

**Track** – in DVD-Audio, a single audio program (i.e. a song or composition). Audio attributes such as channel configuration, sample-rate, and word-length may be changed on Track boundaries (players may mute during such attribute changes).

**track** – in DVD-Video, an audio or subtitle stream which accompanies a video stream.

**UDF** – see Universal Disc Format.

**Universal Disc Format (UDF)** – the file system used in DVD; designed specifically for use on replicated optical media.

**Universal player** – a player with the capabilities of both a DVD-Video player and an Audio-with-Video DVD-Audio player.

**Variable Bit-rate (VBR)** – a video encoding method in which more bits are allocated to complex, hard-to-encode segments of the program, and fewer to the rest, resulting in higher subjective playback quality at lower overall bit-rates.

**VBR** – see Variable Bit-rate.

**Video Manager (VMG)** – a master directory for the data elements on a DVD-Video disc.

**Video Object (VOB)** – the basic media file of DVD-Video presentation data; a multiplexed stream containing the video, audio, and subpicture material to be displayed on screen.

**Video Object Set (VOBS)** – the collection of VOBs which makes up the presentation data referenced by a Video Title.

**Video Title (VTT)** – a single video presentation; part of a Video Title Set.

**Video Title Set (VTS)** – the video, audio and graphical elements of each program on a DVD-Video disc. A VTS is made up of a VTS Menu (VTSM) and one or more Video Titles (VTT). All the video in a given VTS must be in the same aspect ratio.

**Video_TS** – the file directory on a DVD where DVD-Video data are stored.

**VMGM** – Video Manager Menu; the main menu for a DVD-Video volume; the destination of the TITLE button on a DVD-Video player remote.

**VOB** – see Video Object.

**volume** – the top level of organization on a DVD disc. A single-sided DVD (DVD-5 or DVD-9) contains a single DVD volume, while a double-sided disc (DVD-10 or DVD-18) is made up of two independent volumes.

**VTS Menu (VTSM)** – the menu for each VTS on a DVD-Video disc. VTSM is the destination of the MENU button on the player remote.

**WebDVD** – Microsoft's approach to supporting Web-connectivity for DVD; uses the ActiveX-based Windows Media Player and requires a Windows 98 computer with DirectShow decoder and Internet Explorer 5 or higher.

**WG-4** – the working group within the DVD Forum that developed the specifications for DVD-Audio.

**widescreen** – aspect ratios used in film (1.85:1, 2.35:1) and television (16:9) in which the horizontal screen dimension is significantly greater than the vertical.

**workgroup** – an approach to production system design in which a set of workstations, each optimized for specific tasks, is integrated into a network that facilitates the smooth progression of projects though the various stages of production.

# Index

# ⓕ Focal Press

## http://www.focalpress.com

Join Focal Press On-line

As a member you will enjoy the following benefits:

- an email bulletin with **information on new books**
- a bi-monthly **Focal Press Newsletter**:
    - featuring a selection of new titles
    - keeps you informed of **special offers, discounts and freebies**
    - alerts you to **Focal Press news and events** such as author signings and seminars
- complete access to **free content** and reference material on the focalpress site, such as the focalXtra articles and commentary from our authors
- a **Sneak Preview** of selected titles (sample chapters) *before* they publish
- a chance to have your say on our **discussion boards** and **review books** for other focal readers

Focal Club Members are invited to give us feedback on our products and services. Email: worldmarketing@focalpress.com – we want to hear your views!

Membership is FREE. To join, visit our website and register. If you require any further information regarding the on-line club please contact:

Emma Hales, Promotions Controller
Email: emma.hales@repp.co.uk
Fax: +44 (0)1865 315472
Address: Focal Press, Linacre House,
Jordan Hill, Oxford,
UK, OX2 8DP

## Catalogue

For information on all Focal Press titles, we will be happy to send you a free copy of the Focal Press catalogue:

**USA**
Email: christine.degon@bhusa.com

**Europe and rest of World**
Email: carol.burgess@repp.co.uk
Tel: +44 (0)1865 314693

## Potential authors

If you have an idea for a book, please get in touch:

**USA**
Terri Jadick, Associate Editor
Email: terri.jadick@bhusa.com
Tel: +1 781 904 2646
Fax: +1 781 904 2640

**Europe and rest of World**
Christina Donaldson, Editorial Assistant
Email: christina.donaldson@repp.co.uk
Tel: +44 (0)1865 314027
Fax: +44 (0)1865 315472